Faith, Stories and the
Experience of Black Elders

Dementia Services
Development Centre
University of Stirling
STIRLING FK9 4LA

of related interest

Spirituality and Ageing
Edited by Albert Jewell
ISBN 1 85302 631 X

Spiritual Dimensions of Pastoral Care
Practical Theology in a Multidisciplinary Context
Edited by David Willows and John Swinton
Foreword by Don Browning
ISBN 1 85302 892 4

Spirituality in Mental Health Care
John Swinton
ISBN 1 85302 804 5

Spirituality, Healing and Medicine
Return to the Silence
David Aldridge
ISBN 1 85302 554 2

Spirituality and Art Therapy
Living the Connection
Edited by Mimi Farrelly-Hansen
ISBN 1 85302 952 X

Faith, Stories and the Experience of Black Elders

Singing the Lord's Song in a Strange Land

Anthony G. Reddie

Jessica Kingsley Publishers
London and Philadelphia

First published in the United Kingdom in 2001 by
Jessica Kingsley Publishers Ltd,
116 Pentonville Road,
London N1 9JB,
England
and
325 Chestnut Street,
Philadelphia, PA 19106, USA.

www.jkp.com

Library of Congress Cataloging in Publication Data
A CIP catalog record for this book is available from the Library of Congress

British Library Cataloguing in Publication Data
A CIP catalogue record for this book is available from the British Library

ISBN 1 85302 993 9

Printed and Bound in Great Britain by
Athenaeum Press, Gateshead, Tyne and Wear

Contents

Foreword

I was delighted when the author kindly invited me to write a foreword to this book whose subject is surely unique on this side of the Atlantic.

I was first introduced to Anthony Reddie through his ground-breaking Christian education programme *Growing into Hope* in 1998. I then heard about his PhD studies and his subsequent thesis, 'The Christian Education of Black Children in Birmingham'.

My own position at the time was that of pastoral director at Methodist Homes for the Aged, which is the elder-care arm of the Methodist Church. In this capacity I led seminars in the spirituality of ageing with theological students at The Queen's College, Birmingham, amongst other places. I was also responsible for setting up a Centre for the Spirituality of Ageing in Leeds where one of our concerns was to produce resources both for churches and for social and health care professionals. This we saw as being partly fulfilled through the publication of user-friendly versions of suitable academic research which could make a significant impact upon the delivery of social, medical and pastoral care.

I met with Anthony at Queen's and asked if his own research could be presented in a form that would encourage intergenerational working which would affirm the unique contribution of Black elders and provide some kind of paradigm for use in other communities. This book shows how well Anthony Reddie has fulfilled that brief.

It seemed to me that the book was of such value that it should be published mainstream rather than by an organisation with a more limited market potential. Jessica Kingsley Publishers, who in 1998 published a book I edited, *Spirituality and Ageing*, were more than willing to do so, for which readers will be grateful.

I have always been fascinated by the composite life-stories of older people and the particular 'stories' that make them up. Such stories never simply belong to an individual in isolation although they do help to give meaning to that person's life and will tend to be 'quarried' for new significance in the changing circumstances of the life-cycle. They will be shared at least in part with others, most often family members, friends and colleagues. Some stories belong to a whole local community. One thinks of Aberfan devastated by the mining-slip of 1966, or of the Lockerbie air disaster of 1988, or of the school massacre in Dunblane in 1996.

Others are generational. Although the experience of those who lived through the 1939–45 War will contain many variants, nevertheless there are commonalities shared by those who experienced, say, the London blitz or the exigencies of rationing.

Until the early 1960s most young men in Britain experienced a period of two years' National Service. Older people getting together are apt to reminisce about such shared experiences! They can also be in demand in schools where their stories help to transform a potentially dull subject into truly 'living history'.

Yet other stories belong to very large groups of people, whether national, ethnic or of a particular faith tradition. In some cases all three are combined in one. Jews have a very strong sense of identity which is rooted in the 'meta-narratives' of their scriptures, which reinforce their belief that they have been chosen by God, rescued by him from captivity in Egypt and later in Babylon, and restored yet again to 'the Promised Land' in modern times. The old stories are told and retold from generation to generation in a virtually unchanging form, and for them to 'remember' in this way has the very strong sense of identifying them personally and existentially with formative events of aeons ago.

In a similar way, Black people of Caribbean origin in the United Kingdom have suffered from slavery and colonialism within the African diaspora and it is not surprising that their story re-echoes the significant narratives of the Hebrew scriptures and the New Testament Christians who faced marginalisation and persecution which deeply tested their faith. The stories of the elders, keepers of their tradition, interact with, are informed by and feed upon the overarching story of their people. In this way their identity as a group and as individuals is affirmed and significant values are passed on to those who are younger.

Anthony Reddie is aware that disjunction and dislocation threaten this time-honoured process, as do the competing value systems of the pluralist society in which we live, but he accepts this as a challenge rather than as a fait accompli about which nothing can be done. His highly original and non-threatening approach, which is very affirming of the role of older people, is surely one that can be emulated with profit amongst other groups in our progressively fragmenting society, including families, local communities, churches and other faith groups. Dr Reddie provides some eminently adaptable tools for the job.

Albert Jewell
Senior Chaplain, Methodist Homes

Acknowledgements

In thanking the many people who have helped this book to come to fruition, I must begin by acknowledging the lively presence of countless numbers of Black elders. These individuals, with whom I interacted for some eighteen months, provided the raw materials that assisted in the creation of this book. I feel something of a fraud when I remember the countless hours spent in church meeting-rooms and the front rooms of many of these people, recounting stories from the past. How could something so enjoyable, so life-affirming and undoubtedly beneficial to my own identity and growth be called work? I would like to thank all the many Black elders with whom I met during my time with the Birmingham Initiative for your fellowship, warm hearts and your yet to be equalled cooking. I am a better and a fatter person for having met all of you.

Having mentioned the Birmingham Initiative in the last sentence, I need to thank the management committee of the project, particularly the chair of the committee, for the support and encouragement I received whilst undertaking this work. Undoubtedly, the experience of working on this project changed my life.

I am indebted to the Revd. Albert Jewell of Methodist Homes for the Aged who suggested that I write this book based on my research. I still remember his beaming face and unbounded sense of excitement as I described this section of my research to him. That kind of enthusiasm is life-affirming and should be bottled. Thanks are due also to the Pastoral Care and Christian Office of the Connexional Team of the Methodist Church, particularly the Children's and Family and Personal Relationships sections.

The Queen's Foundation for Ecumenical Theological Education, particularly the Research Centre, deserves thanks for allowing me the space to undertake the necessary revisions to the text upon the completion of my doctorate.

Finally, and perhaps, most personally, I would like to thank my parents for having nurtured and supported me throughout the whole course of my life to date. Theirs has been a story of self-sacrifice and vicarious pleasure, having witnessed the faltering yet sure-footed progress of their four children. We have all had the opportunity to undertake and accomplish things of which they could barely dream. Their thirty-five-year stay in this country was largely unspectacular and they are known by a comparatively small circle of people. Yet to me they have been my world and I owe them everything. I know that they have taken pleasure in the things my three siblings, Richard, Christopher and Sandra and I have achieved. This knowledge is the most satisfying and pleasing aspect of the work I have undertaken. Noel and Lucille Reddie now live in Portland, Jamaica, and I am proud to be their son.

Introduction

This book is based upon the doctoral work I undertook whilst working for the Birmingham Initiative from 1995 to 1999. The Birmingham Initiative was a Methodist-inspired, ecumenical research project that was concerned with the Christian education and nurture of African Caribbean children in inner-city churches in Birmingham. The research was conducted amongst twenty-six inner-city churches of the Methodist, Anglican, Baptist and United Reformed Church (URC) traditions.

Whilst the work of the project was concerned primarily with the teaching and learning of the Christian faith amongst Black children, it was clear from the start that this work needed to be earthed within the experiences of the wider framework of Black family life. One could not attempt to work with Black children without reference being made to the older members of the family. These older members, often grandparents, were and continue to remain the bedrock upon which Black family life is lived in twentieth and twenty-first century Britain.

Given the initial focus of the research, it was not possible to investigate the claims and the importance of Black elders in their own right. Despite being conscious of the needs and importance of this pioneering set of people, my research at that time did not afford me the opportunity to take this interest any further. At the back of my mind, however, there lay a dormant thought, namely, that this work must not be forgotten or allowed to disappear.

The '*Windrush*' generation that are at the heart of this book are now in their dotage. As the ravages of time and chronology exercise their inevitable judgement, many of these pioneers are returning home, some to their cultural and spiritual home back in the Caribbean and in Africa, others to the ancestral home in the next life. Whichever of the two eventualities has befallen them, it is vitally important that we acknowledge and affirm the achievements and the steadfastness of these epic heroes and heroines of an almost forgotten time. For without their brave and courageous spirit, many of my peers and I would not be here today with the opportunity to express our experiences in writing. I am painfully aware of the irony that tinges the whole enterprise of this book. I am writing (and indeed have the opportunity to write) about the experiences of my elders and forbears, who themselves were often denied the opportunity to tell their own story: their story of singing the Lord's song in a strange land.

This book, in one sense, has emerged at a strange time. It is almost a case of 'after the Lord Mayor's parade' ... In many respects, the most opportune time for the celebration of the black presence in Britain seemed to be some years ago back in 1998. 1998 was a momentous year for this country, as we celebrated the fiftieth anniversary of the landing of the SS *Empire Windrush*. This ocean liner brought the first postwar migrants from the Caribbean to Britain. In the following two decades close to a million people would join them. Our presence has enlivened a monochrome country.

But 1998 has gone and with it the plethora of television programmes, books and exhibitions that were commissioned, often for the first time, to mark our presence. Contrary to the opinion of a former prime minister of this country, we have not swamped this nation with an alien culture. If our moment in the sun has gone, why is this book being published now?

I believe there are two reasons that make this publication a timely one. First we need to be reminded, continually, that the presence, contributions and achievements of Black people, particularly, Black elders, are ongoing ones. They cannot and should not be restricted to one-off events in the nation's consciousness. Are we to wait another fifty years for our next moment in the sun? The recognition of Black people in Britain and within the church during 1998 was an important moment for us all. Black people have not suddenly disappeared, however, and our presence needs to be noted and affirmed on a continual basis. Hence, the timely nature of this book.

Secondly, I feel this book makes an important contribution to the growing literature on the Black presence in Britain. Whilst a number of publications have been written, not least as a part of the 'Windrush' celebrations, very few of these pieces have dealt with the religious and spiritual dimension of Black people. Black people are incurably religious. A belief in powers higher than the temporal, mortal realm of humankind, lies at the very heart of our understanding and relationship to the created world order. The struggles of our ancestors in Africa and in the Caribbean were forged in relationship with a belief in the benevolent power of the Creator. The stories of our travails and triumphs are contained in the narratives of these people throughout the ages.

In this book I have attempted to investigate the oral sources of Black experience, in order to use these traditions to affirm Black elders living in Britain, and to educate their young counterparts for the journeys that await them. It is intended to be a resource for individuals, churches, social work and other agencies that have contact with Black elders in Britain, in whatever context.

This work incorporates three broad approaches. The first part of the book contains my academic work, which attempts to establish the historical and theological background of the oral traditions of Black people – the very traditions which have given rise to the stories of faith and experience that are demonstrated in the book. The second part outlines the methodology and framework I created and later implemented in order to gain access to these stories of faith and experience. I hope that this framework and method will assist those working with Black elders to identify opportunities and strategies by which they can enable these individuals to share their stories and the experiences for the benefit of all. The third and final section attempts to highlight some of the implications and possibilities arising from this work. I hope that you find this book of interest, and a practical resource for your work.

The book begins with a dramatic sketch, which attempts to encapsulate the initial experiences of Britain for many of these Black elders.

'Looking ahead'

A dramatic sketch

The scene: Inside a church we see about half a dozen West Indians sitting in a pew, waiting for the service to begin. The setting is some time in the early 1960s.

Man 1: Where is that preacher man? Late as usual.

Woman 1: Dem always late.

Man & Woman 1: Late late late late late.

Man 1: [*To Man 2*] Leonard, how is your new house shaping up?

Man 2: Shaping up nice.

Woman 1: What your neighbours like?

Man 2: Me don't know, dem nuh speak to me yet.

Man 1: How long you been there now?

Man 2: Six months and still not a word. Some of dese people funny you know. Last week, me did go out into the garden to say hello to my neighbour. Guess me what dis 'oman did when she see me?

Woman 1: Is what she do?

Man 2: Me say guess.

Woman 1: Hmmm ... Invited you in for a cup of tea?

Man 2: Noh talk foolishness ... You cyan guess? Well, when she see me, she pick up her bundle of washing, all her belonging, grab her pickney and dash back into the house. She t'ink me go'n eat her or somet'ing.

Woman 1: Dem t'ink we like de taste of white flesh.

Man 2: Well back home I used to eat missionary pie every Friday.

Man 1: [*To Man 3 and Woman 2*] How is yu two? You alright?

Man 3: Just perfect.

Woman 1: [*To Woman 3*] Is how yu white neighbours?

Woman 2: Me don't have noh white neighbours. One week my family move in, next week, three a dem move out. I'm sure I don't smell, I bathe everyday.

Man 3: My neighbours are fine. Very friendly. Dem talk to me all de time. Only de other day, dis nice man ax me how long I go'n stay in this country. So I tell him, five years. He's a very nice man. Always talking to me.

Man 2: What sort of things do you talk about?

Man 3: Everything. De weather. My stiff bones. How come it rains nearly everyday. How come de English are always singing about a white Christmas? Dat mek no sense. If it snows, then your bones freeze up more and de buses stop running. How yu get anywhere? And why do de English queue fe everything? We never queue back home. The man with the biggest fis' always get what he want. And how come this country have no summer? Den there's de price of green bonanas. How comes they so expensive over here, when dey cost us nothing back home? Why won't they let me live in a nice neighbourhood or get a good job? Why haven't they got a batsman as good as Sobers? As I said, everything.

Woman 1: Strange country. I miss back home yu know.

Man 1: Me too. The sun never shines over here. You cyan call what dem get over here sunshine. When I first come over ya so, all me had to my name was one felt hat and a cotton shirt. Come the winter, man, me nearly dead. Now back home, dat is what I call sun … [*Slight pause*] … shine.

Everyone: Yeah man, sunshine.

Enter about half a dozen young children. They are the Sunday School. They walk to the front.

Man 1: At last, de preacher … [*pointing to the children*] Isn't dat your boy, Leonard?

Man 2: Dat's him. Handsome looking bwoy. Clever as well you know. I think Brian go'n be famous. Just you watch him.

Woman 2: Dat's my boy next to him. Anthony. If he didn't misbehave so much, he could do something with himself. Needs some discipline. Some stiff lick in his …

Man 3: [*Interrupting Woman 2*] Don't forget yu is in church.

Woman 2: Well I still say he needs some discipline.

Woman 1: And dat's my Carol. Too quiet fe her own good.

Man 2: Which one Carol again?

Woman 1: De one standing next to Susan.

Man 2: Susan, now dat is one noisy chil'.

Preacher begins to talk. The congregation are all quiet. Preacher lines up the children in front of him/her.

Preacher: Let the little children come to me, and do not hinder them, for the Kingdom of God belongs to such as these ... [*begins to talk directly to the children*] You are the future. I hope your shoulders are strong. For it will be you who will take on the load in future years. You must all work and study hard and be a credit to your parents. [*points to congregation*] Do you see your parents out there? [*All the children begin to nod.*] Well, they have travelled long distances and made great sacrifices to give you a chance. Chances they never had. You're not going to let them down, are you? [*All the children shake their heads.*] Good ... [*looks at Brian.*] Tell me Brian, what do you want to do when you grow up? Tell the congregation.

Brian: I'm going to be a musician.

All the other children laugh.

Brian: [*Turning to everyone else*] What are you lot laughing at?

Carol: You, a musician?

Brian: I will so.

Carol: You won't.

Brian: Will.

Carol: Won't.

Brian: Will.

Carol: Won't, won't, won't.

Brian: Will, will, will.

Both of them begin to fight. The preacher breaks it up.

Preacher: Now that's enough of that. If Brian says he will, then he will ... Won't you, Brian? [*Brian nods.*] And what are you going to do, Carol?

Carol: Don't know.

Preacher: No ideas?

Carol shakes her head, Brian begins to laugh and Carol slaps him.

Preacher: [*To Susan*] What are you going to do when you grow up?

Susan: Be a nurse like my Mum.

Preacher: That's wonderful. Susan is going to be a nurse. You're not scared of the sight of blood are you?

Anthony: Susan's a vampire. I've seen her drinking blood.

Susan turns around and slaps Anthony.

Preacher: And Anthony, what about you?

Anthony: I'm going to be an engine driver, or an astronaut. Or maybe a fireman. Or a footballer, or a teacher, or a film star, or a boxer, or a runner, or a cricketer, or a soldier or a ...

Preacher: [*Putting hand over Anthony's mouth to shut him up*] You obviously have a very active imagination, Anthony. [*Turning to Mary*] And what about you, Mary?

Mary: I'm going to be a Minister, like you.

Preacher: The hours are long and the pay is lousy ... [*Looking up*] May God continue to bless these children as they grow and may they be a credit to all of us. For the future belongs to all of them. Amen.

The preacher and children go back to their seats.

Man 1: [*Slight pause*] You see Brian. Dat's fe my bwoy.

Woman 1: I just wish Carol would have something to say for herself.

Woman 2: I just wish Anthony would have less to say for himself. Dat bwoy has no idea whatsoever. Not a piece of sense.

Man 3: So Susan's go'n be a nurse? Clever girl, Susan.

Man 2: It's good when children have ambition. After all, dat's why we come to dis dey cold country in de firs' place. To give our children de bes' chance. Shame 'bout Mary, though?

Woman 2: Why?

Man 2: You t'ink a clever girl like dat would know better. Who ever hear of a Black woman becoming a preacher? Her mother should have a strong word with her.

Man 1: Quiet yourself, Leonard. Let the girl have ambition. Someone has to be successful, so why not Mary? Dese children can do anything. Just you watch them.

Woman 1: Dey can do anything dem want, so long as dey have ambition. I wish I was their age again. Den maybe my bones wouldn't be so stiff. Dis cold weather no joke you know. England must be one sinful country fe God to punish her like dis.

Man 3: What yu mean, punish her?

Woman 1: Den is where de sunshine? How come it cold all de time? If dat noh God's judgement, den show me what is?

Woman 2: [*Clapping hands together, trying to keep warm*] I could love dis country if it wasn't fe de cold.

Man 2: If wishes were horses, den beggars would ride.

Man 1: Maybe if we all close our eyes and pray together, de Lord might tek pity on us.

Man 3: We have nothing fe lose.

All five of them stand up, hold hands and close their eyes.

Everyone: Lord have mercy, and send us some sunshine.

After a five-second delay, they all open their eyes.
Woman 2 licks her finger and puts it high into the air.
She then shakes her head.

Everyone: Cold!

Where it all began

The sketch you have just read was written nine years ago. The occasion that prompted me to write this piece was the impending visit of Ivan Weekes, the then Vice-President of the Methodist Conference (an elected office, which represents the highest position of honour that can be afforded to a lay person in the church). Ivan was scheduled to attend my home church, Moseley Road Methodist, for a (Birmingham) district celebration event, as part of his semi-nomadic wanderings around the Methodist Church for that year. I, along with a group of young (or at least, younger than we are now) adults at the church was charged with the responsibility of devising a programme of entertainment for that evening.

Very early in the planning stage, I was asked if I could write three short dramatic sketches, based upon the experiences of Black people in Britain. After much thought I decided to base my pieces on the past, present and (largely positive, one hoped) future experiences of Black people living in Britain. In the development of my writing these pieces were of huge significance, for they were the first attempts to write explicitly about Black people. Prior to this I had usually written my scripts and stories from what I have termed a 'spurious universalism'. By this term I mean to suggest that my writing was notionally geared to everyone and the characters within the pieces were largely nondescript, vague and very, very fictional. They spoke in a general, universal language, about general, universal things. These people spoke for everyone, but in truth spoke for no one. These people were generic, universal people, who in truth were nobodies.

You see, there was no context, no 'interior' to these stories and the people who populated them. There were no accents, no quirks of behaviour and no cultural reference points prompting you to exclaim, 'I know that person!' All that changed when I wrote 'Looking Ahead'. For the first time, I began to write about people, situations and contexts that were familiar to me. These people were my people. Their stories were my stories.

When I wrote 'Looking Ahead', I drew upon the stories and anecdotes of my parents, aunties and uncles and the wonderful people who inhabit my church, many of whom had become almost second parents to me since my own birth parents returned to the Caribbean in 1991. I looked into the eyes of these individuals, drew upon my memories and recollections, and began to write. What emerged is 'Looking Ahead'. Were it not for 'Looking Ahead' and this seismic breakthrough, there would have been no *Growing into Hope* (Reddie, 1998b/c), nor the cultural, Black perspective on Christian education, practical theology and spirituality that emerged through the research and writing I undertook with the Birmingham Initiative.

I have chosen to commence this book with 'Looking Ahead', because it encapsulates what, for many, were the formative experiences of being Black, largely coming from the Caribbean, and living in Britain in the late 1950s and early 1960s. The sketch touches upon a moment in time for that group of people who are now termed 'the *Windrush* generation'. (See Reddie (1999) and Freyer (1984). These two pieces offer insights into the historical development of postwar Black immigration to Britain, and the experiences of these Caribbean migrants in Britain since the landing of the SS *Empire Windrush* on these shores in 1948.)

The importance of these individuals to the life of my own church and that of the many inner-city churches up and down the country is evidenced by the changing complexion of these institutions over the past twenty-five years. It has become increasingly the case that, were it not for the for-bearance, faith and obstinacy of these individuals, such tra-ditions as Methodist, Anglican, Baptist and United Re-formed would no longer have any worshipping congrega-tions in inner-city areas in Britain. The greater majority of the worshipping congregations of inner-city churches are comprised of these older, fiercely proud, yet supremely loving and accommodating Black people, many of whom came to Britain from the Caribbean in the 1950s and 1960s. These people who were once overlooked and often despised have now become the fulcrum and bedrock of these churches. 'The stone that the builders refused has now become the head cornerstone.'

This sketch serves as an introduction to my book and a reminder to this country, and the many churches and inner-city faith communities within these shores, of the struggles of older Black people. In order to understand the stories of faith and experience, to which reference is made in later chapters, one needs to have a sense of the contexts from which these narratives have emerged. These contexts are ones of poverty, struggle, pain, hardship and a grim determi nation to create a better life for one's offspring. When Man 2 in the sketch remarks that they came to Britain in order that their children might have greater opportunities than those afforded them, herein lies one of the most basic truths of Black migration for the past 150 years. People have moved in order to create a new life for themselves and their children. People have left homes, loved ones, familiar spaces and worlds, moving to new pastures, in order that a new exist-ence might become a reality. African and Caribbean people have never been 'little Islanders' or 'little villagers'. We are people who, from the smallness of our immediate surroundings, have always envisaged a huge world. We believe that we have been accompanied on our travels by a huge God, as we have moved from one context to another, struggling to create the 'new' in strange, often unpromising environments. (See Reddie (1998a). In this article, I discuss my understanding of family, using my own familial experiences as my first point of departure. In this article, I refer to the migratory impulse of Black people, who since the dawn of the twentieth century, have travelled from their places of birth, in order to create new lives and develop fresh experiences in contexts radically different from the ones in which they were first nurtured.) The experiences of these older Black people are hugely important, for they provide the foundation for the post-Second World War, mass Black presence in Britain.

To understand the present, we need to return to the past – to return to the era of the 1950s and 1960s, and the time of early struggle. In many respects we need to retreat even further back in time. We need to travel to the Caribbean. In the final analysis, we need to return to the continent of Africa. For the stories of faith and experience to which you will be exposed have their origins in Africa, in the era that predates slavery. But before we engage in reverse time-travel, let us reflect for a moment.

Re-read 'Looking Ahead'. What have you learnt about these people, and their struggles and hopes? What became of their children? What became of them? What are the links between the migratory travels of Black people and the children of God in the Old Testament? What can we learn about God and the Old Testament scriptures through reflecting upon the life experiences and struggles of these older Black people?

I believe that this sketch could provide the basis for a very interesting discussion in a discussion, fellowship or Bible study group.

1

Developing a new approach

This book is aimed at a wider audience than those who are familiar with, or possess some commitment or allegiance to, the Christian faith and the varied traditions of the Christian Church that seeks to live out the truths that are intrinsic to Christianity. It must be understood, however, that in order to understand Black people best, particularly Black elders, one needs to have some sense of the importance of matters of faith in the ongoing existence of people of African descent. The cosmology of African people is one in which a divine Creator is at work within the whole world order. While the spiritual dimension of African people can be expressed in myriad forms, I have chosen to approach it and reflect upon it within a Christian framework. It is my belief that a large pro- portion of Black elders would express an actualised belief in God, and a resulting Christian faith, which represents a constant presence and an affirming reality in their lives. I would hazard a guess that this proportion would be consid- erably higher than any corresponding figure for Christian faith amongst any other section of British society.

To understand my fascination with the oral reminiscences of older Black people we have to return to the work that I undertook on behalf of the Methodist Church when work- ing on the Birmingham Initiative. The Birmingham Initiative was a Methodist-inspired, ecumenical research project that was concerned with attempting to create a new example or model for the Christian education and nurture of Black children in inner-city churches. In this research, I was hoping to develop a new approach to the strategy by which people are taught the Christian faith. Of equal importance is how the process of learning about God's love for human-kind, as demonstrated in the life of Jesus Christ, can lead to the transformation of the individual.

One of the major outcomes of the doctoral research I undertook was the creation of two volumes of Christian education material entitled *Growing into Hope* (Reddie 1998b, 1998c).

In the final stages of completing the text of *Growing into Hope*, an additional theme emerged within the research. As I will explain later, the development of this piece of work owed much to the creation of the Lent and Easter material in this Christian education text (Reddie 1998c, pp.12–133).

The attempt to create a new model for the Christian education of Black children in inner-city churches had been heavily dependent upon devising and implementing teaching and learning materials. In the course of conducting the final phase of the piloting and implementation process that was to give rise to *Growing into Hope*, I was concerned that a significant area in the ongoing experiences of Black people remained unexplored. My attention was drawn towards the informal, more oblique forms of Christian education and spiritual development that emerge primarily through the medium of the family. What I have in mind are the examples of Christian living that arise through the family and the interactions among its various constituent members; also its dialogue with the past through familial remembering and folklore, and its engagement with the present.

My awareness of the importance of grandparents in the spirituality and Christian education of Black children was not a recent phenomenon. Throughout my ongoing work with the various churches, the importance of oral traditions within the familial structure of Black life was never far from my mind. In the first instance, I was aware that the importance of Black family life and the role of intergenerational discourse or conversation in the nurturing and development of an individual's spirituality were concerns expressed by the funders and originators of this research project.

In the planning and consultation phase that preceded my appointment as the research worker, a number of possible outcomes were formulated for the project. Amongst the many expressed hopes was the desire that the research should be

> People-based, not just concentrating on resources – concerned with Christian education and nurture in church and home, for individuals, groups and families, all ages, for the whole church community throughout the week, not just based on Sunday. (Reddie 2000, Vol. 2, p.37)

On commencing the research I was faced with a number of practical problems when trying to find a means of gaining access to the private experiences and stories of Black people. One of the major difficulties lies in the differences between Black experiences and cultural traditions, and the overall white, Eurocentric norms that govern many inner-city Anglican, Methodist, Baptist and United Reformed churches, and indeed wider British Society. (See Reddie (2001/2), Wilkinson et al. 1985, John 1976 and Walton 1985). These differences have led to a sense of alienation and disaffection amongst Black people towards these particular institutions and wider British society. This alienation and disaffection are manifested, to an even greater extent, in the behaviour and attitudes of Black children.

Given the divided nature of Black identity and expression, it seemed unlikely that I would be able to gain access to the private domain of these Black elders. Given that such limitations were in place, I could not conceive of a means by which I might gain access to the homes of Black people as stated in the preliminary outline document from which I quoted above. Consequently, it was agreed that a more practical method of working should be employed, namely, to concentrate on the more public space of the church and the resultant Christian education work that is undertaken in junior church/Sunday schools.

The shift from written curriculum to oral-based approaches was to prove something of a struggle. It was not until the early months of 1998 and the largely successful deployment of the Christian education material that I felt sufficiently confident to attempt an important change of direction. This change represented an attempt to engage with the oral traditions of people of African descent. From the outset of the research I had attempted to acknowledge the importance of oral traditions and narrative within my curriculum writings. On a number of occasions I encouraged adult Christian education leaders to exhort their Black learners to solicit their respective parents and grandparents for responses to particular questions. (See Reddie 1998b, 1998c.)

When creating this material, I was mindful of the thoughts of many commentators regarding the importance of the Black family in diasporan African life. Allen (1982), Aschenbrenner (1980), Hill and Shackleford (1986), Roberts (1980) and Sudarkasa (1981) have all expounded in differing ways upon the importance of the Black family in the ongoing experiences of people of African descent. Hannah appraises the importance of the concept of Black extended families. He describes some of the central features of these models of African-centred patterns of intra-communial family, and continues by stating

> The cohesion exemplified by the extended family's inter-connectedness is yet another reflection of its grounding in African heritage. In African society, emphases are placed on tribe members' horizontal relationships with relatives

currently living, and vertical relationships connecting ancestors and those family members yet to be born. (Hannah 1991, p.44)

The concept of the family in Black life is hugely important. Particular emphasis must be placed upon those older members who made the long journey from the Caribbean in the post-Second World War migration of the last century. These older individuals remain important for their continued commitment to inner-city Methodist, Anglican, Baptist, URC, Pentecostal and Catholic churches. Were it not for their tenacity, diligence and strength of faith, these churches would no longer exist. The importance of these individuals increased following the departure of the White middle-class from the inner cities (Reddie 1999).

The importance of older Black people lies in the direct link between these individuals and the Caribbean. The greater majority of these individuals were born in the Caribbean. Their experiences, family narratives and stories of faith are potentially vital resources for enabling Black children to discover aspects of their identity. Hazareesingh offers a useful methodology for enabling young children to elicit family stories from their parents. In addition, she posits a useful rationale for these forms of familial remembering. This model propounded by the author involves young children interviewing parents and grandparents, asking questions of older family members about their place of birth, upbringing and other related matters (Hazareesingh 1994). Hazareesingh believes that this method has an important role in enabling minority ethnic children to reclaim their cultural heritage and so forge a more positive identity that reflects the rich variety of their ancestry. Speaking of this process, Hazareesingh says, 'Grandparents' accounts of their memories of the past – their own experiences or events they have witnessed – can take children back a stage further' (p. 29).

My contacts with a number of the older Black men and women in these inner-city churches had alerted me to the important element of narrative and folktales in the lives of these individuals. Having witnessed at first hand fragments of the experiences and aspects of faith of some of these individuals, I felt it was necessary to investigate further, into the history and the theory that might lie behind the life experiences of Black elders. What are the oral traditions of Black people, and from what contexts and settings have they emerged? This leads us into the next section.

The oral tradition of African people

Ella P. Mitchell describes the oral tradition of Black people as being the summation of the cultural vehicles through which the essential nature of Black existence and experience has been channelled. These cultural vehicles assist African people in their knowledge of self, both individually and corporately. They are manifested in many forms, ranging from storytelling, festivals, celebrations, parties, role-play and acting, through to religious worship. The origins for these communicative modes of cultural transmission are to be found in Africa (E.P. Mitchell 1986).

According to Vansina, this oral tradition can be subdivided into a number of categories or classes. These range from memorised messages that are represented in a formulaic manner (prayers for example), through to more informal structures such as folk tales and proverbs (Vansina 1985). Phillippe Denis makes the point that oral traditions are inherent within African people and the societies from which they emerge (Denis 1995). Denis distinguishes between oral history and oral traditions. Oral history comprises hearsay or eyewitness accounts of events of a contemporary nature.

These events have usually taken place within the lifetime of the informants providing the oral recollections. Conversely, oral traditions are not contemporary, but have been passed on by word of mouth over an extended period beyond the lifetime of the informant.

These traditions not only come in a variety of forms as intimated by Mitchell and Vansina, but they are also the most natural and powerful of discourses. The powerful nature of oral communication lies in the reciprocity that is inherent within most forms of conversation. If one is speaking, most usually one is speaking to or with another person. Eye contact and body language are two factors that assist in creating a sense of mutuality in oral transmission. Orality has immediacy and fluidity. It is neither fixed nor immutable. Text, on the other hand, is often the antithesis of all the aforementioned. It does not require an audience to read it. Most often when the author was composing that text he or she did so as a solitary being, removed from the potential audience of readers (Berryman 1991, p.70).

Writers such as Prins have noted that attempts by European historians to document the historical developments of the African continent have relied almost solely upon written documents, written texts produced by westerners operating within a colonial environment (Prins 1991). Prins questions the alleged objectivity of these accounts, noting that the perception of Africa from these text-based offerings was 'The view from the district commissioner's verandah or the mission compound' (Prins 1991, pp.217–18).

The seeming primacy of text has been challenged in more recent times by a number of historians and anthropologists who have asserted the importance of oral sources, as has Paul Thompson, stating that 'I am not dependent on any one author, but on countless faithful witnesses who either know or remember the facts, part from what I know myself' (Thompson 1988, p.28).

The importance of oral history as a radically alternative form of understanding one's identity through accessing the facility and function of shared memory is explored by a number of anthropologists. (See Connerton 1989, Tonkin 1992 and Werbner 1998.)

It is not my contention that African people are alone in possessing an oral tradition. Clearly, there are many ethnic and religious groups who possess oral traditions that are the repository of experience, and which provide the narrative thread of biography and existence. I would argue, however, that this facility has played a particularly important role in the ongoing life experiences of African people.

I make this contention aware of the central importance of Black theology and the aim of that discipline to affirm and legitimate the Black experience as a valid source for talking about God's interaction with God's people. James Cone says,

> There is no truth for and about Black people that does not emerge out of the context of their experience. Truth in this sense is Black truth, a truth disclosed in the history and the culture of Black people. Black theology is a theology of and for Black people, an examination of their stories, tales and sayings. (Cone 1975, pp.17–18)

Cone continues by suggesting that these experiences and expressions, often crystallised in stories, folk sayings, the spirituals, the blues and in sermons, cannot be subdivided into secular and religious. Rather, they sit alongside each other in a unitary whole of human experience (Cone 1975, p.23).

Michael Goldberg acknowledges Cone's importance in the development of narrative approaches to theology:

> For Cone, the stories of the Bible combine with the stories of the Black experience to offer an alternative vision of the ultimately distorted and distorting view of reality reflected in the tales told by whites. (Goldberg 1982, p.16)

Goldberg is a proponent of a narrative approach to theology. He argues that biography and autobiography are important sources for the theological understanding of the individual and whole communities. Within the life stories of individuals there is a presumption of some notion of truth (Goldberg 1982, p.64). Narrative theology offers us a way of understanding the nature and the truths of God, within the context of the stories of faith and experience of the individual or the corporate believer.

The development in my own understanding of the oral tradition of African peoples was assisted by an exploration of biographical and autobiographical faith stories in particular and narrative theology in general. In terms of the latter, the work of James Fowler was to prove instructive. (See Fowler *et al.* 1980.) Fowler *et al.* outline a hermeneutical framework for investigating the lives of individuals, from which one can derive a sense of the development of faith across a whole life. Fowler writes:

> Telling the stories of saints and heroes is a universal feature of religious life. Insights into the personality of a great teacher and a narrative that gives the full context of the teacher lend a note of authenticity to the records of instruction. (Fowler 1980, p.9)

The work of Fowler and that of other scholars in the area of developmental theories on human faith construction is more concerned with the *how* than the *what* of faith (Goldberg 1982, p.89). In short, the primary focus of their work is directed at how people construct particular patterns of understanding ultimate questions of existence, rather than the substance of that faith itself. Nevertheless, I found a number of insights that assisted me in developing this area of work. The oral traditions of Black people are located within the narratives of these people of faith. Arising from these narratives are multitudes of theological connections. One needs to be conscious of the resulting links these individuals make between their individual experience, the corporate whole of which they are a part and the God whom they profess to worship. These links provide the raw materials that can affirm and assist a younger generation in their emotional and psychological development.

With reference to narrative theology Goldberg analyses the ways in which human beings derive some benefit from linking their own personal stories with Biblical narratives. He states that

> These narrative theologians not only understand such stories as being true portrayals of past events, but also as a ringing true to some common aspect(s) of human experience, thereby providing the basis on which human beings might more truthfully live their lives. (Goldberg 1982, p.244)

Josselson and Lieblich argues that stories which operate within the framework of an individual's life are important, for they provide opportunities for the individual subject to construct explicit meaning for that person (Josselson and Lieblich 1993, p.18).

The importance and the function of the oral tradition

Fred Lofton asserts the importance of an oral tradition within the life experiences of Black people. This tradition was passed down in an intergenerational form through storytelling, and was one of the primary means by which Black people survived the dehumanising experiences of slavery (Lofton 1991, p.127). The oral tradition provided a necessary filter against the disinformation and lies that were told in order to demonise and humiliate Black people. This demonisation of the African psyche was propagated by

White slave owners and White authority. These biased, self-serving efforts at discrediting Black people were often given validity by text, such as the Bible. The narrative of Genesis 9 for example, and the so-called 'curse of Ham', has been used by European scholars to justify the oppression of African people on the grounds that Ham can be identified as being the progenitor of all Black, African people. By making this rather imaginative and spurious link, one can identify Black people as being cursed by God (via Noah), and therefore deserving of whatever fate might befall them.

The biased, self-serving use of text to humiliate and subjugate Black people could be countered and challenged by African people accessing their oral tradition. Robert Beckford says something to this effect in *Jesus is Dread* (Beckford, 1998). When talking of Bob Marley as a Black Liberation Theologian, he states, 'Real knowledge for Marley must be validated by experience. Experience is the filter which enables us to find meaning in the world' (Beckford 1998, p.118).

Colleen Birchett states that, historically, most Black people gained their Christian formation from an oral tradition that was expressed in a dual form: initially, on a Sunday in the pastor's sermon; second, through instruction and storytelling from the family during the remainder of the week (Birchett 1989, p.74).

The development of Christian education curricula and accompanying strategies for teaching the Christian faith to Black people are more recent innovations in Black majority churches. Grant Shockley is of the opinion that formalised, text-based Christian education programmes only came into prominence in Black majority churches at the beginning of the last century (Shockley 1989, p.236). Prior to that time, an oral tradition that consisted of experience, both individual and corporate, and was expressed through storytelling was the usual means by which the Christian faith was passed on from one generation to the next.

In the first instance, Ella P. Mitchell inspired me to take seriously the oral nature of African people. As one who is by nature a writer, I was greatly challenged by Mitchell. I realised that it was important not to fall into the western, post-enlightenment trap of believing allegedly objective rational text to be superior to the claims of experiential, subjective forms of knowledge (E.P. Mitchell 1986, p.111). Mitchell reminded me that for the majority of Black people the Christian faith has been caught, not taught (E.P. Mitchell 1986, p.102).

Our overemphasis upon text serves to mask the central importance of oral communication and the power within that form to inspire, transform and energise. As Berryman reminds us, the two most influential people in western philosophical thought have been Socrates and Jesus Christ, and neither individual is recorded as having written anything (Berryman 1991, p.64).

It was the thoughts suggested by Mitchell that led me to think explicitly about orality in Black life, when writing part of the Christian education curriculum related to Mothering Sunday (Reddie 1998c, pp.15–38). This material in *Growing into Hope* was to prove the basis for the later developments in the oral tradition work of Black people. Having outlined the theoretical background of this work, there remained the next task, that of talking to Black elders, to see how this translated in reality. This issue will be discussed in the following chapter.

2

Speaking with Black elders
An early attempt

My first attempt at gaining access to the often private stories and experiences of Black elders came through a meeting with a group of older Black people. Meeting these Black elders was to prove a huge turning point in my research.

This breakthrough came when I was invited to speak to a fellowship group (or a nurture group, for want of an alternative term), in one of the participating churches in the research project. This church is situated in the north part of Birmingham. The membership of this Methodist church is predominantly Black, with the greater majority of members being in their sixties and seventies. Most of these individuals came from the Caribbean in the post-Second World War mass migration of Black people from the New Commonwealth to Britain.

Upon meeting these older Black people, I attempted to engage with the women (and one man) in order to assist them in supporting and encouraging their grandchildren in the Christian faith. These individuals informed me about their experiences of growing up in the Caribbean. Through hearing their stories, I began to gain a clearer understanding of how these varied contexts had shaped both the experience and the expressions of faith of these Caribbean women. Many of them had a secure and grounded sense of their own identity. In stark contrast to their grandchildren, they remembered with great vividness being nurtured in secure environments where they experienced a very real sense of belonging. Many of them spoke of the church in the Caribbean, and of their role and participation within that setting as being one where they felt truly affirmed. I will return to this session at a later point in this chapter. The practical schema that was created in order to stimulate intergenerational conversation arose from this session.

I had gained a sense of the dynamics of this facet of Black experience by means of this conversation with Black elders in this inner-city church. In the presence of these individuals I witnessed active, lived examples of Black theology. Black theology, in the context of this work, is an understanding of God, which is expressed in and through the reality of Black experience and struggle. This form of Black theology is a dynamic relationship with God, in which meaning and hope (which are indispensable facets of life for Black people in a world that is governed by White people with power) are found in the figure of Jesus Christ – God's beloved son, who came in order that all (with particular reference for all Black people and those from the so-called two-thirds world) might have life more abundantly.

There has been much controversy surrounding the notion of Black theology. There are many who find this discipline too esoteric and abstract. Yet in the very narratives of these Black elders were templates for a grounded conception of the Christian faith that was authentic and shorn of pomposity and pretence. It was this form of conversation shared freely with an academic researcher that I hoped to facilitate in familial settings between differing generations of Black people. The individuals in this group would vehemently have disavowed any notion of their discussion being the substantive elements of Black theology. I remain convinced, however, that the substance of these narratives contains the antecedents of the liberation struggle of Black people in postwar Britain at the dawn of a new millennium.

The conversations with these women centred on their reminiscences of childhood and being nurtured in the Caribbean. My initial question (replicated in the oral tradition document in the form introduced and documented later in this book) concerned their memories of the oldest person they had met in their family. I asked the group to share an anecdote concerning these individuals. The greater majority of the group spoke of parents and grandparents who exacted discipline and commanded respect in a manner that might be frowned upon in more recent era. I asked Nancy, a seventy-something Black woman, for her memories of growing up with her mother in rural Jamaica.

Nancy [speaking about her mother]: I was 'fraid of getting a beating so I just do my work. I scared of licks so much. And if we at school come home with a complaint, we get another one. My Mummy would say, if you never did anything then teacher wouldn't have reason to beat you … [There is much laughter and agreement from the others in the room.] So you see, these kids get away with murder these days. When me tell my granddaughter, little ****. When me tell **** how my mother could beat me. She said, 'Grandma, you should a kick her one.' [There are huge howls of laughter from the other people in the room.] I said girl, if you was in my mother's days. But she said, 'But grandma, you a kick her one and then she wouldn't have done you all that.' [There is more laughter.] I got too many my dear. [Too many memories of corporal punishment to think that she could have acted any differently than she did at the time.] My mother! That's why I loved me Dad. Dad couldn't throw a straight cap at me. [More howls of laughter.] But me Mum? If even a month pass she still a beat you. She never forget a beating. And me still love her you know.

Nancy's account of her stern Mother is typical of myriad accounts of maternal discipline in Caribbean households, and the importance of respect for elders. The group in this session was aware of the significant differences between the nurture of children in the Caribbean and that of their own grandchildren in this present context. In hard, often unforgiving times, it was paramount that children be instructed at the earliest opportunity to understand the unremitting realities of colonialism and injustice. These contextual realities are echoed in Ella P. Mitchell's writing on the oral traditions of African Americans dating back to the era of slavery. Mitchell delineates the importance of children learning quickly from adults about the harsh realities of life. Mitchell writes:

> The gravity of the plight was obvious, and slave parents dared not try and protect their offspring from hard reality. The best evidence of this fact is the sophistication among small children in dealing with situations where survival was at stake. (E. P. Mitchell 1986, p.103)

The realities of their upbringing and nurture had exerted a profound influence upon these Black women. From such circumstances had emerged particular values, traditions and norms of behaviour that often sit uncomfortably in our present time. None of these women had attempted to replicate the exact nature of their own childhood upon their children or grandchildren. There was a realisation that in a different context those behavioural forms and attitudes would not be appropriate. The seeming clash between different cultures and contexts is hinted at in one of the proverbs in the Mothering Sunday material for the oldest group, which is detailed in a previous publication (Reddie 1998c, pp.34–35). The twelfth proverb in the list, and the one that caused a great deal of discussion, states that parents should 'Spare the rod and spoil the child'.

The discourse from this meeting reinforced many of the central themes that had emerged in my earlier research looking at the role of proverbial wisdom in African and Caribbean communities in Britain and around the world. This form of proverbial wisdom is expressed in wise sayings, figurative aphorisms and storytelling. A number of academics are beginning to look at the educational potential for proverbial wisdom, particularly that which emerges from the Hebrew scriptures (Melchert 1998). Indeed, scholars such as Randall Bailey have made direct links between the wisdom tradition of the Hebrew scriptures and the proverbial wisdom of people of African descent (Bailey 1991).

One of the important issues that arose in these early conversations was the question of respect for one's elders within the family and the wider community. The importance of respect for all people older than oneself and for one's ancestors is a theme that is replicated throughout African societies within continental Africa and across the diaspora. (For further information on this matter see Du Bois 1965; Diop 1974; Hale-Benson 1986; Hale 1994; Raboteau 1978; Mbiti 1970, 1975; Shorter 1978; Asante and Asante (eds.) 1990.)

Selvie, a Black woman in her early sixties, recounted the importance of respect for elders in the following account. Her story also offers us an insight into the proverbial quality of Black storytelling. The resulting moral to this story is self-evident.

> *Selvie:* You were talking about your elder brother. [Speaking to the rest of the group.] You always had to have respect for your older brother and older sister. Anybody you had to have respect to. So it was like me and my second and third eldest brother and we went to school and as usual it was like [a phrase has been missed as the words were inaudible] in those times in Jamaica. And errm, we went to school except

for my brother paid for the dinner, cos we used to have dinner at school, a cooked dinner. We as kids you know we would say that you craven [greedy].[1] A' craven you craven. We used to have this something they call salt-dog it's like fried dumplin, with salt-fish in it, and we'd call it salt-dog [a traditional Caribbean dish, referred to in other islands of the Caribbean as 'bakes']. And it used to be nice at break time, with drops [candy drops] and something like that. Because of cravenness my older brother says what do you want for dinner? Do you wanna stay for dinner or do you want to buy salt dog and drops and all that? So me and my other brother said let's buy salt-dog for dinner. And my poor older brother you know just buy it and with syrup and things like that. So we eat it. And we was happy and it was nice. By time we out school we belly start hurt. We start fe barl 'Auntie, My belly a' hot [hurt][2] me. Auntie, me belly a' hot me.' So she ask 'What did you eat at school?' [Begins to cry out like a little child who is telling tales]. 'Auntie, **** [her older brother] buy us cake and salt-dog and syrup and t'ing.'

Miriam:	[another Caribbean woman in her sixties]: And he only bought you that 'cos you ask for it.
Selvie:	And a craven we craven why we belly a hot we. And my poor brother got told off for buying us all that. He was older than us, you know ...
Anthony:	He should have known better?
Selvie:	He never done it again. He just pass out the money and make us eat dinner. I enjoyed my childhood.
Nancy:	I enjoy my childhood. It was lovely. Was the best time of my life.

This extract is indicative of the anecdotal form in which the narratives of these Black elders are often couched. Selvie's reminiscences indicate the responsibilities that were placed upon the eldest child. This form of responsibility remains an important factor in diasporan African life.

Selvie's anecdote offers us an insight into the mechanism of proverbial wisdom. It highlights the invaluable lesson her older brother learned regarding the importance of responsibility. There are times when an act of misplaced benevolence can rebound upon the recipient, leading to further trouble in the future. Similarly, this incident taught Selvie the importance of not being 'craven'. The importance of not being 'craven', which served as one of the morals in this story, is reflected within a previous publication that arose from this research (Reddie 1998c, pp.142–4).

Daniel and Smitherman outline five important areas of analysis for proverbial wisdom and folk tales, the third of which relates to the impact of this form of oral tradition upon the development of the child. They argue that

> Proverbs are central to mental development and abstract thinking and reasoning – training in proverbs can supplement formal education, particularly in the area of critical thinking. (Daniel and Smitherman 1976, p.35)

This early session with Black elders was critical, in that it enabled me to gain an insight into some of the experiences that had shaped this group of individuals as people. While the dramatic sketch at the beginning of 'Looking Ahead' attempts to encapsulate aspects of the early experiences of many Black people arriving in Britain in the 1950s and 1960s,[3] this section seeks to return those actors to the Caribbean. One cannot understand Black elders (nor elders belonging to any ethnic or sociological grouping) without the elders themselves, and those who work with them, making the necessary journey into the past.

This session marked my attempt to visit the past, albeit very briefly, with a group of loquacious Black elders. It was a truly inspiring occasion. In the next chapter I will detail the process by which a systematic approach to eliciting the oral traditions of Black elders was achieved.

Notes

1   See Volume Two of *Growing into Hope: Liberation and Change*, p.142. In the story 'Greedy Bwoy Learns a Lesson', the word 'craven' is used by the mother to admonish her son for his excessive greed, which lands him in trouble.

2   This expression is a popular colloquialism in the Caribbean. Its approximate meaning is to be in great pain.

3   'Looking Ahead' was drawn from the myriad conversations I have had with older Black people, many of whom have had experiences similar to my own parents. It is a concentrated form of memory.

3

Creating the oral
tradition document

In the previous chapter I described my first significant opportunity to speak with a group of Black elders. I wanted to assess the effectiveness of their stories as possible resources for supporting the nurturing of spiritual development, faith and the general socialisation of their grandchildren. Having completed this first session, there remained new mountains to climb if the work was going to progress.

My first session with a group of Black elders had developed largely through accident and coincidence. My previous dealings with these individuals had enabled this session to take place.[1] In order to develop a strategy that might lead to consistent opportunities to gain access to the stories and experiences of Black elders, I needed a framework that would enable older Black people to speak with confidence.

In pursuit of my goal of developing a mechanism that could support the oral tradition amongst Black people, I was indebted to the work of Anne Wimberly. In her book *Soul Stories*, Wimberly sets out a framework she describes as 'story-linking'. This is offered as an intergenerational tool for sharing experiences in an oral form. Wimberly says of her method:

> The story-linking approach will invite your reflection on positive and problematic contemporary stories. Particularly, you will be invited to consider how liberation and vocation

are exhibited in the stories and how liberation and vocation are inhibited. (Wimberly 1994, p.21)

Wimberly's story-linking approach, particularly in its attempt to link individual narrative with the lives of heroic people of faith, is not wholly dissimilar to that adopted by Fowler (Fowler *et al.* 1980).

Although extremely helpful as a resource, the story-linking process could not provide a contextualised method for sharing oral traditions amongst Black people in the British situation. A number of Black academics (Bruce 1976; Curry 1991; Frazier 1964; Stokes 1974) have argued that the continuity between African Americans of differing generations has been provided by the ongoing reality of the Black experience housed, most notably, within the bedrock of the Black Church. The institutional Black Church in the United States offered a safe space and became a refuge against the unremitting travails of racism and discrimination that were unleashed upon Black people. This continuity of experience has been both the process and the product of an oral tradition that is a vibrant and an effective means of social, political and Christian education.

Wimberly accepts this legacy of faith within the African American experience as being the norm, and bases her approach upon this reality. For Black people in Britain, particularly African Caribbean people, there is the double discontinuity of their separation from Africa. The first was achieved through the forced removal through the epoch of slavery. The first exilic period was followed some four centuries later by the postwar departure from the Caribbean. The latter can be described as a voluntary form of migration, fuelled by economic necessity. One cannot assume a continuous, uninterrupted thread of experience and cultural transmission that surmounts differing contexts and diverse, plural settings. In blunt terms, some of us have been away from the ancestral home for a long, long time, and there is considerable doubt as to whether we can ever return to the location in an unchanged fashion.

In order to create a practical tool to encourage an explicit rendering of the oral tradition in Britain, it was essential that I sought to adapt Wimberly's method. Additionally, I wanted to utilise the work of Joseph V. Crockett. Crockett states that

> Telling stories from one's cultural legacy allows for entrée into the world and the lives of learners … By telling stories of one's cultural heritage, a teacher has the potential to crack open the doors and make contact with significant aspects of the learner's existence. (Crockett 1991, p.6)

The resulting document that emerged from my ongoing research was entitled 'Sharing Experiences Between People of Different Generations', and was an attempt to traverse the diverse contexts of diasporan African life. This approach aims to provide a framework in which experiences, traditions and values from one particular location (Africa and the Caribbean) can be shared, and upon which, in due course, one can improvise and adapt for a radically different context (inner-city Britain).

It was my hope that this document would facilitate the telling and sharing of stories. The experiences of surviving, overcoming, adapting and ultimately, for some, triumphing, is recorded within the narratives of Black people. This legacy of faith, as depicted by Robert E. Hood, has given rise to a distinctive expression of Christianity (Hood 1990, pp.13–87).

Janice Hale, commenting on the importance of African stories of experience, says:

> These stories transmit the message to black children that there is a great deal of quicksand and many land mines on

the road to becoming a black achiever ... They also transmit the message that it is possible to overcome these obstacles. These stories help black children de-personalise oppression when they encounter it and enable them to place their personal difficulties into the context of the overall black liberation struggle. (Hale 1995, p.207)

The substantive content of some of these stories is given in the next chapter. These examples are preceded, however, by the Oral Tradition document, the full text of which is contained in the following pages.

Sharing experiences between people of different generations

There is a two-fold aim to the following material. First, it provides a structure that will enable caregivers, health care professionals and lay people or non-professional individuals of faith to engage in conversation with the elders of their communities, particularly those who are Black. The following document is an attempt to facilitate a structured form of reminiscence work and storytelling, which will affirm Black and other elders. Second, this document is intended to assist parents, grandparents and other guardians of Black children in sharing traditional stories of faith, personal experiences and reflections from their own life with a younger generation that is present in most inner-city churches. The material is concerned, primarily, with the oral transmission of faith – the way in which one generation of Christian believers has sought to pass on its experiences and wisdom to succeeding generations – thereby helping their 'inheritors' to learn from their example.

In most cultures and societies an 'oral tradition' is often in evidence. In such elements as folklore, traditional sayings such as proverbs (see the 'Mothering Sunday' material of the

'Lent and Easter' section of Volume Two of *Growing into Hope*) and other forms of reminiscences, we see how values and beliefs in any society are passed on from one generation to succeeding generations. This aspect of human existence is no less a powerful force in the lives of Black people living in Britain. For hundreds of years the lived experience of the Christian faith has been passed on through storytelling and example.

This new material before you is mainly directed at enabling 'structured' conversations between Black people of differing generations. The most natural setting for this material is any place where grandparents, parents and children and young people meet, share experiences and interact as 'family' in an informal way. The material, however, can be used in other settings. In residential care homes, hospitals, after-school clubs and elders' support or fellowship groups, this structure can be used to bring people of different ages together, in order that stories of faith and experience can be shared.

The role of adult children's workers (Sunday school teachers if you prefer), ministers, pastoral visitors and social workers is paramount in this particular framework I have created. In the context of this work their role is to assist in this process, enabling these important remembrances and experiences to be shared between people of different generations. It is important that these workers see the implementation of this work as part of an ongoing process. Administrators and practitioners need to facilitate opportunities where older people and children can review the outcomes and the fruits of their conversations. What has been learnt? What new pieces of learning have emerged? Children and young people should be encouraged to bring and share the fruits of these important conversations with their peers in the church, school or after-school club setting. For those within a church context, I would suggest that one Sunday in the month (or something approaching that frequency) be set aside for children and young people to share some of their experiences. A similar structure or provision can be made in those settings where many of our elders are offered care and support.

One practical suggestion related to this area is taken from the 'Words and Stories' part (the Second Sunday in Advent) of the 'Advent' section in Volume One of *Growing into Hope*. The children and young people in the 'middle' and 'oldest' groups can be encouraged to draw 'family trees', beginning with great-grandparents (if they are still living), and finishing with themselves and their siblings and cousins. The children's workers/leaders should then encourage the children and young people to go through their family trees, describing the different members of the family. What is their grandmother like? How would they describe their grandmother's personality? Are they similar? Can they remember one story about their grandmother? What is their favourite memory? These are a few of the questions you could ask, encouraging the children and young people to share their experiences.

The aim is to assist the children and young people to reflect upon these experiences in order to understand how they have been influenced by their parents and grandparents and to see how they are similar or different, and how they might learn from the older members of their family. This will give these children and young people a greater sense of 'where they come from' – their 'roots' and the family history of which they are a part. (You will need to exercise caution, however, in using this method/document, as some children and young people may live with adopted or foster parents, and may be sensitive about looking at family history.)

Alternatively, for those working with elders, a similar process can be used, beginning with the family tree. For pastoral workers and ministers in church it may be appropriate on a number of occasions to invite an older member of the congregation to share some of their experiences with the children and young people in the junior church or within the main worshipping service on a Sunday. The individual asked to share their experiences can be asked to reflect upon their upbringing. What was their grandmother/father like? What is their earliest memory? Can they remember one story from their childhood which is important to them? Why is this story important?

Through all this, it is important that the practitioners (of whatever guise) themselves gain a greater understanding of the influences and traditions that impact upon the lives of Black elders and their younger counterparts. This under-standing will undoubtedly assist such individuals to relate to those with whom they work in a more informed fashion.

I hope you find the sample questions on the following pages helpful in assisting people of different generations to engage in intergenerational conversations.

SHARING EXPERIENCES
BETWEEN PEOPLE
OF DIFFERENT GENERATIONS
(THE ORAL TRADITION DOCUMENT)

Introduction

THE FOLLOWING QUESTIONS ARE DESIGNED FOR ELDERS TO SHARE THEIR EXPERIENCES AND CHRISTIAN FAITH WITH YOUNGER ADULTS, CHILDREN AND YOUNG PEOPLE. THE QUESTIONS ARE ONLY MEANT TO SERVE AS A GUIDE. PLEASE FEEL FREE TO AMEND AND ADAPT THEM IN ORDER TO MEET YOUR OWN REQUIREMENTS.

It may be helpful to have a tape recorder to record the answers you give. It will be helpful to come back to these answers at a later date.

All the following eight sections take the form of three questions. The first question in each section is directed at the OLDER PERSON (a grandparent, parent or some older guardian). The second question is directed at the CHILD /YOUNG PERSON. The third question is for both the OLDER PERSON and the CHILD/YOUNG PERSON to look at each other's answers, in order to look for any similarities.

The grandparent or elder should begin by inserting their name at the appropriate place in the family tree. The oldest people should be at the top of the page and the youngest people at the bottom. Alternatively, you can draw your own family tree. The enclosed diagram a fairly simple Family Tree to assist you, but please feel free to create your own.

The following process may need to be adapted if the older person and the younger person are not related or do not know each other very well.

Sample family tree

Put names to the categories below (where are you?)

	great grandparent grandparent(s)	
great aunts & uncles		great aunts & uncles
uncles & aunts	parent(s)	uncles & aunts
cousins	children	cousins

1. About older persons

For the older person:

(a) Who is the oldest person you remember in your family?

(b) What was that person like?

(c) Tell one story you remember about that person.

For the child/ young person:

(a) Who is the oldest person you remember in your family?

(b) What was that person like?

(c) Tell one story you remember about that person.

For the child/ young person:

(a) What do you remember about the person your grandparent/ parent described? (What they said.)

(b) Does this person sound anything like you?

(c) How are you the same?

Older persons:

(a) What do you remember about the person your young relative described?

(b) Did you know or meet this person?

(c) Is, or was, this person anything like you?

(d) How are you the same?

Now see what each of you has said:	*What things are the same or nearly the same between both of you and the two people you have described? (e.g. height, looks, personality etc.)*

2. About parents and grandparents

Older persons:	(a)	*What is your earliest memory (or one of your earliest memories) of your father or mother or grandmother?*
	(b)	*Say one thing you have learnt from this person.*

For the child/ young person:	(a)	*What is your earliest memory (or one of your earliest memories) of your father or mother or grandmother?*
	(b)	*Say one thing you learnt from this person.*

Now see what each of you has said:	(a)	*Is there anything the same, or nearly the same, that you have both learnt from your fathers or mothers or grandmothers?*
	(b)	*Is there anything the same, or nearly the same, about what you both remember?*

3. Being young ourselves

Older persons:	(a)	*What was the best thing about when you were very small or very young?*
	(b)	*Can you think of one moment or time when you were really happy, when you were very small or very young?*

For the child/ young person:

(a) *What was the best thing about when you were very small or very young?*

(b) *Can you think of one moment or time when you were really happy, when you were very small or very young?*

Now see what each of you has said:

(a) *What things are the same or nearly the same about when you were both very small or very young?*

(b) *What is the main difference?*

4. Troubled times

Older persons:

(a) *Can you think of one time in your life when you were in trouble or you had a problem?*

(b) *How did you overcome or solve the trouble or problem?*

For the child/ young person:

(a) *Can you think of one time in your life when you were in trouble or you had a problem?*

(b) *How did you overcome or solve the trouble or problem?*

Now see what each of you has said:

(a) *Is there anything the same or nearly the same about how you solved or overcame your problems or troubles?*

5. Praying

Older persons:

(a) *Do you pray when you have problems or troubles?*

For the child/ young person:	*(a)*	*Do you pray when you have problems or troubles?*
Now see what each of you has said:	*(a)*	*How do you pray?*
	(b)	*What sort of things do you say?*
Older persons:	*(a)*	*Have you learnt anything about prayer from either (i) the oldest person in the family (go back to the first question) or (ii) from a grandparent or parent?*
	(b)	*If yes, what things have you learnt?*
For the child/ young person:	*(a)*	*Have you learnt anything about prayer from either (i) the oldest person you remember in your family (the person in the first question) or (ii) from a grandparent or parent?*
	(b)	*If yes, what things have you learnt?*

If the child or young person has not learnt anything (or at least they claim they have not or cannot remember), the adult can take this opportunity to share with them what they have learnt.

Now see what each of you has said:	*(a)*	*Is there anything the same or nearly the same about what you have both learnt about prayer?*

6. Looking to Jesus

Older persons:	*(a)*	*When you are praying, what is Jesus like in your prayers?*

| | (b) | How do you imagine or picture him? (e.g. is Jesus tall or short? Is he like anyone in your family?) |

(c)   Say one thing you like about Jesus.

(d)   What is your favourite story of Jesus in the Bible?

(e)   Why do you like that story?

For the child/ young person:

(a)   When you are praying, what is Jesus like in your prayers?

(b)   How do you imagine or picture him? (e.g. is Jesus tall or short? Is he like anyone in your family?)

(c)   Say one thing you like about Jesus.

(d)   What is your favourite story of Jesus in the Bible?

(e)   Why do you like that story?

Now see what each of you has said:

(a)   Is there anything the same or nearly the same about what you like about Jesus?

(b)   Do you like the same stories?

7. Learning about Jesus from each other

Older persons:

(a)   Have you learnt anything about Jesus from either (i) the oldest person you remember in your family (the person in the first question) or (ii) from a grandparent or parent?

For the child/ young person:

(a)   Have you learnt anything about Jesus from either (i) the oldest person you remember in your family (the person in the first question) or (ii) from a grandparent or parent?

| Now see what each other has said: | (a) | *Is there anything the same or nearly the same about what you have both learnt about Jesus from older people in your family?* |

> If the child or young person has not learnt anything (or at least they claim they have not or cannot remember), the adult can take this opportunity to share with them what they have learnt.

8. Hope for the future

| Older persons: | (a) | *What are your dreams for the future?* |
| | (b) | *Can you think of one way you can make one of your dreams come true?* |

| For the child/ young person: | (a) | *What are your dreams for the future?* |
| | (b) | *Can you think of one way you can make one of your dreams come true?* |

Now see what each other has said:	(a)	*Are your dreams the same or nearly the same or are they different?*
	(b)	*How are they nearly the same?*
	(c)	*How are they different?*

> Ask the child/young person (if they are not too embarrassed) to say a short prayer for the OLDER PERSONS.
>
> The adult then says a short prayer for the CHILD/ YOUNG PERSON.

Notes

1   Prior to my appointment as the Christian Education Worker for the Birmingham Initiative, I had spent three years as a Youth and Community Worker for two inner-city Methodist churches in the Asbury circuit in Birmingham. The membership in both of these churches was mainly Black. The Black elders who contributed to this session are members of one of the two churches.

4

Piloting the oral tradition document

Intergenerational work with families

The piloting of the oral tradition document took place within three inner-city churches in Birmingham. Within each of the three churches chosen to be a major respondent for the oral tradition phase of the research was one particular family which I identified as being significant within the life of that respective faith community. I do not claim that these families are in any way representative of the whole faith community to which they belong.

The families with whom I chose to work were highly respected members of their various faith communities. Each played a significant role within the life of the church. Importantly, the various families were represented within the Christian education work in their church through the presence of the youngest family member.

In reporting this section of the work I have chosen to concentrate, in the first instance, upon one particular family belonging to a Methodist Church situated in the south-west of Birmingham.

This section of the book details my practical attempts to initiate structured, intergenerational conversations between Black people of different generations. The very act of attempting to facilitate these conversations is an important breakthrough in its own right. This is evidenced in anecdotal accounts highlighting the discontinuity in oral traditions of Black people from one context to another, namely, from the Caribbean and Africa to Britain. The discontinuity between diverse contexts is manifested in the seeming reluctance of a number of grandparents to share their familial narratives with their grandchildren.

The comprehensive *1996 Black Child Report* details the wide variance that exists between Black children who share in interesting conversations with their parents (Walker and Biye 1997, p.198). The group least likely to share in conversations with parents are fifteen-year-old males (*ibid.* p.198). The sample group in this large-scale quantitative research is not identical with my own, as the authors' focus is a more generic approach that incorporates all people of African descent (*ibid.* p.2). This research is targeted at Black people who predominate in Methodist, Anglican, Baptist and United Reformed churches in Birmingham. Despite these divergences, however, the *1996 Black Child Report* is instructive for the insights it offers into the cultural milieu in which Black children are socialised and nurtured in this country.

The report highlights the disparity between Black children who are conscious of relatives outside their immediate home and those who are not so well informed about more distant family members (*ibid.* pp.180–3). The development of a positive self-identity is enhanced when individuals are conscious of the familial narratives and the corporate and collective history that have influenced the ongoing experiences of their forebears (Wimberly 1994, pp.22–4). The recognition of the importance of familial knowledge is reflected in the diagrammatic family tree structure in the oral tradition document, in which the first section of questions relating to 'older persons' aims to enable families to discuss Black forebears.

A Black family from the Methodist church at the centre of the research – a case study

I had been in contact with this family for approximately two years prior to our structured conversations on the oral traditions within their family. Initially, my immediate point of contact had been Lesley. Lesley had been baptised as an infant in this church and attended most Sundays with her mother Maureen, her mother's sister Doreen, and Bee, her grandmother. The family was seen as stalwarts of the church. Lesley's presence at church was actively supported by the older members of the family.

All family members occupied some formal role within the church. Bee, the grandmother, was a communion steward and a member of the church council. Maureen was not only a member of the church council, but had recently undertaken the role of church council secretary. Doreen, like her mother and sister, was a member of the church council. Lesley, in addition to attending the junior church/Sunday school also assisted Mary (the regular adult leader) in running the Christian education sessions on a Sunday morning.

I met with this family on 3 May 1998 in the home belonging to the grandmother. This setting was viewed collectively as the family home. The various constituent members of this extended family committed themselves to meeting every Sunday at Bee's home for Sunday dinner. This setting was a compact and affirming context in which the Christian faith was shared amongst the differing individuals of the family. I had arranged to meet them in the afternoon following their Sunday dinner.

I began by asking Bee, who is in her late sixties, about the oldest person she remembered meeting in the family.

> *Anthony (A)* So, Mrs ****, who is the oldest person you remember in your family?

Bee (B)   My grandmother.

A   And what was she like?

B   Very funny in her ways you know. She used to
             make some crude remarks you know, saying all
             kinda old fashioned things. She never really call
             things or words the way they should be. If she
             had to say something she turn it a way, into a
             different thing. When, errm. If she wants to say
             'the same thing', she would say 'A' de same
             t'ing'[1], you know. But we understood her very
             well. And she had a great sense of humour.

A   And can you tell me one story you remember
             about her?

B   She told so many stories. Her stories are always
             about… Well, we say 'duppy'. [*There is a great deal
             of laughter at this term, which in Jamaican creole means
             'a ghost or roaming spirit'.*] But it was always some
             duppy story she was always telling us. And she
             used to come and stay with us in the evenings
             you know. She would leave her house and come
             to us. And then when she finish telling us her
             stories you know, we were scared to go bed.
             Because they're always ghost stories she's telling
             us.[2] Things that happened to her when she was a
             girl. And she never say 'girl', she say [*spelt
             phonetically*] 'gheerl'.

A   [*To Maureen*] So, Maureen, who is the oldest
             person you remember in your family?

Maureen (M) My great grandmother.

A   What was she like?

M   Just as Mum said. She was Mum's granny. Very
             funny. Always had a smile on her face, yeah! And
             she was one for discipline. She was always on

about discipline. 'You must break the tree when it's young.' She was a lovely little old lady.

A   Can you think of one story about her that sums her up?

M   She used to tell us things like, errm. Treatment that they used to use in their day. Not medical treatment. If you had a sore foot you would go and mix up all different things to put on it. And she was a great believer in trying everything. And she was just a unique person. She really was. Sad to lose her.

A So!   Lesley, it's your turn now. Who is the oldest person you remember in your family?

Lesley   My great grandmother. I only saw her once. She was short.

The references to elements of African retentive beliefs in the comments of Bee and Maureen when talking about their grandmother and great grandmother respectively are quite instructive. These women had their formative experiences in Jamaica and were influenced to some extent by this older woman who was born in the latter part of the nineteenth century. This older matriarch possessed of beliefs and traditional skills that emanate from Africa could be some two generations only removed from slavery. Through the power of memory, these older women possessed some form of familial link with experiences and practices that first found expression in continental Africa.

My conversations with Lesley, who was born and socialised in Birmingham, are somewhat different. At the time of our conversation she was sixteen years old. Her first visit to Jamaica, the birthplace of her mother and grandmother, was in 1991, when she was nine. Her memories are somewhat vague about that experience. She has virtually no direct memories of this older Black woman of whom her older relatives speak. Although she has been exposed to conversations and stories about this woman, the world from which this woman emerged is a foreign one to Lesley. Lesley's great, great grandmother is a symbolic representation of a syncretic world where Africa meets the Caribbean. The double discontinuity between Africa, the Caribbean and Britain is reflected in the significant differences between Bee, Maureen and Lesley, from three different generations of Black women.

There were a number of shared notions of selfhood and faith that both united and provided a common thread of continuity between the different generations of Black women. One aspect of their shared commonality was the element of Christian faith. Of particular import was the facility of prayer. I began by asking Bee about her experience of prayer.

A   [*to Bee*] So, Mrs ****. Do you pray when you have problems or troubles?

B   I pray all the times, not only when I have troubles. But I know that prayer is very important. Prayer goes a long way. It will see you through anything.

A   So when do you pray?

B   I pray every day. Sometimes I'm in the kitchen and I'm praying. Sometimes I'm in the toilet and I still pray. At nights I pray. And I pray more so now that I'm on my own. Now that my husband is gone and you know, I pray more now. I find myself praying even more now, because I've been ill and I've prayed a lot for that. Also that God will see me through it and he has. And I pray because I want to thank him for all that he has done for me. [*She begins to cry.*]

A Who taught you how to pray?

B I taught myself. Sometimes I find myself repeating things, but I ask God to teach me about pray. I say Lord, teach me that I can pray. Teach me how to pray and he's answered my prayers.

A And so Maureen, when do you pray?

M At night, mostly. When I'm going to bed. When I set out for work in the morning, I get in the car and I say 'Lord, take me safely to work.' And when I get to work I say 'Thank you.' I do the same when I'm coming home at nights. I get in the car and I ask God to take me safely home. Yeah, and I say thank you.

A So who taught you how to pray?

M Well my grandparents when I used to live with them. And then when I came here I said the prayer they taught me and I was laughed at and taught how to pray properly. [*They all begin to laugh.*] Well it's the truth.

B Tell him what you used to pray.

M You don't want to hear that do you?

A Oh I do.

M Thank you Jesus meek and mild, look upon a little child. Pity my simplicity suffer me to come to thee.³ And then I said 'Pray mumma⁴ ... [*Begins to laugh once again.*] Let me finish. [*Unable to speak due to excessive laughter.*]

A Come on. Come on, Maureen. No no, no, come. Come, come.

M I'm finishing.

B You know, hmmm. One night she be going to bed and I said to her, 'Maureen have you said your prayers?' And she said, 'Yes I have.' So I said 'I didn't hear you so say it now' and she said, 'Gentle Jesus' and that was alright. But then when she finish that she said 'Pray mumma, pray puppa, pray to God to mek me a good child, for Christ's sake Amen.' So I said 'Is that all you goin' say? Pray mumma, pray puppa? Is where you get this prayer from?' That was the word I used. 'Is where you get this here yes kinda pray from?' [*There is a great deal of laughter.*] And she said that's what they taught her to say it at home. [*More laughter*]

M   ...I had to kneel down you hear?

A   So Lesley, do you pray?

L   Yeah.

A   So when do you pray?

L   Just before I go to sleep.

A   So what prayer do you say? Do you say the same prayer your Mum said? [*Laughter*]

L   No. First off, I like pray for my family. Then I like pray for my friends as well. And then I do the Lord's prayer.

A   So who taught you how to pray?

L   I suppose my Mum did. And at my school, it's a church school. They taught me there as well. And then I suppose I learnt at church as well.

A   Would you say that you had as much faith as your Mum?

L   Probably not.

A   What makes you say that?

L   I don't know. Sometimes when she talks, like when we went to my cousin's christening, and she started talking about the christening, and then she went into say 'May God look after him'. And I was thinking if I was doing that I probably wouldn't have said all of that.

A   Do you think it's to do with age, or do you think it's just that your mum's more religious than you are?

L   Probably a bit of both!

A   So, Maureen, would you say that you have as much faith as your Mum?

M   It's very difficult to say. I don't know. We haven't really sat down and discussed our faith as such. I'm sure there's certain things she probably believes in more than I do. There are certain things I might think more of than she. So it might balance itself out. I don't know. We haven't discussed it.

A   [*to Bee*] So, Mrs ****, would you say that your mother, was she a religious person?

B   My mother? Yes she was.

A   So would you say that you were influenced by her a great deal, in terms of going to church and trying to be a Christian?

B   Yes I was. Because as a small child she always see to it that we go to church and, the Bible, we had to read it. And like I said before, singing. I was always singing. And she always make sure that we do that.

A   Let me ask a question to all of you. And anyone can answer. Would you say that God answers prayer?

In unison Yeah.

M   Definitely.

B   He does, he does.

A   How do you know that?

M   How do I know? There are things I've asked him for, I pray and it's happened. And more recently I know that Lesley was taking an exam at school and I know that she was worried about it, and I prayed, and asked God to help her and her friends to understand the question and to get her through it. And she passed. So, I know that God answers prayers.

A   [*to Bee*] Mrs ****?

B   He answers prayers because when I pray I ask him to help me to accept the things I cannot change. To change the things I can. And the serenity and the judgement to understand. And he's given me those things. Because when **** was sick [*referring to her husband, who died of cancer a few years prior to this interview*] I pray, and I thought Lord, I cannot change his illness, but please Lord, help me to accept it. Of course he gave me the courage and the knowledge to accept it. And I couldn't talk about it one time. I couldn't talk about it. If the television programme come on the telly about it, and providing he's in there, I used to come out the room, or sometimes pretend as if I want to see something else, because I didn't want to talk about it. But after praying, I found that I could leave the television on and we could talk about it openly, and I wasn't scared about talking about it. And I thought well, God is really working in me. [*She begins to cry.*]

At this point Doreen, Lesley's auntie and the younger sister of Maureen, asked if she could enter the proceedings. She had hitherto chosen to be silent. As her mother began to speak about prayer, particularly as it related to the cancer that had killed her father, she felt it appropriate that she share a few words with the rest of her family. Doreen is a professional woman in her mid-thirties, some ten years younger than Maureen. Like her niece Lesley, she was born in Britain as opposed to Jamaica.

> *Doreen (D)* I was just gonna say that talking about praying and the way that God answers your prayers and whatever, Mummy was saying about when Daddy was ill and Mummy accepted it. But, I think through prayer that Daddy learnt to accept it. Because for a long time Daddy used to get, it was obvious that he was scared. He was scared of the cancer. He was scared because he knew that he was going to die. And none of us could talk about it. Nobody spoke about it. And then, I mean I know that, especially on a Sunday Daddy would be upstairs. Towards, towards the end, when he'd be upstairs in bed, I don't mean in the latter weeks or months. And I'd go up and sometimes he'd just be sitting there. He'd either be sitting looking at himself in the mirror. The wardrobe has a mirror. Or, sometimes he'd just be crying. And, I used to say to him 'Do you want me to read the Bible for you?' And he'd say yeah, and there was no specific passage. I'd just open it and read, wherever or whatever it was on. And as time went by, it was obvious that Daddy came to accept it and he wasn't scared anymore, and he used to talk about it, and he'd make the odd joke, you know. Like, [*mimicking her father*] 'When me gone, unno⁵ not gon' know wha' fe do.' And he made preparations. Somebody that's scared and doesn't believe in God, I think that would be, especially a black man. A man as well, would just not be able to cope the way Daddy did. And you

> know he made his preparations. Daddy had
> everything, absolutely everything arranged.

M   Everything.

D   If Daddy had died today and none of us were
> here, a stranger, you could come in, Anthony, and
> everything would be there, prepared and you'd
> know what to do. Short of leaving you know, like
> a note saying an itinerary, everything was there.
> And I think that was because Daddy believed and
> trusted in God. Like he believed and trusted in
> the doctors. He believed and trusted in God, and
> he knew that God was going to end his suffering
> in whatever way. And he knew that it was going
> to result in death, and he accepted it. And I think
> that was the power of prayer.

Prayer was an important resource for all members of the
family. For Bee, the matriarch of the family, it helped her
come to terms with the death of her husband. Prayer was an
equally vibrant resource for her now departed husband.

The world from which Bee and Maureen gained their
formative influences is one that is highly religious and less
secular than the British context of the early twenty-first
century. The Caribbean of the 1950s and 1960s was passing
through a colonial, pre-independence era of extreme
poverty and struggle. (See Williams 1970, Hall 1981 and
Randle 1993.)

For the greater majority of peoples living in the diverse
islands of the Caribbean, liberation from the concrete
realities of poverty and marginalisation emanated from the
Church. This identification with the Christian faith as a
means of liberation has a historic dimension. Bee and
Maureen's literal appropriation of prayer as a means of overcoming contextual struggles finds echoes in the actions and
beliefs of slaves on the Caribbean islands.

Kortright Davis asserts that slaves never accepted a transcendent construct of God as remote and above the sufferings of Black people. Conversely, the slaves held onto a concept of an immanent God that was alongside them in their struggles (Davis 1990, p.59). Davis continues by reminding us that African people believe strongly in the immediacy of supernatural beings that exist alongside ordinary human beings in their common existence (*ibid.* p.59).

I believe it is hugely important that we attempt to use the experiences of older Black people to assist in the nurture and development of their younger relatives. I believe that the work I have highlighted, aside from the important insights it offers into the experiences, the theological and cultural issues and themes that have shaped the Christian faith of these individuals, has implications for our generic work with elders in Britain.

What I hope has emerged from this chapter is the importance of accessing the stories of experience of Black elders (and all elders for that matter), as they offer us a window into a world that was. A world to which we may not be able to return, but one nonetheless that continues to exert a profound sense of meaning on the present and the possible future. In short, access to that past, by means of the narratives of our elders, can enable us to gain a clearer sense of our present identities, and the sacrifices and struggles that were undertaken in order that this present could exist in its familiar form. The implications and applicability of this work will be explored in the final section of the book.

Notes

1   An example of a Jamaican creole variant on what might be termed normative or standard English.

2   These forms of folk narratives that speak of roaming spirits and ghosts are elements of African retention which are in part a product of the syncretism

between traditional African religions brought principally from West Africa by transported slaves and the Christian faith taught to these incarcerated persons by the white slave plantocracy in the Caribbean and the Americas. (*Note:* 'white slave plantocracy' is an academic term referring to the oligarchy of landed White colonial masters, who either owned or oversaw the slave plantations in the Carribean.) A detailed explanation of these religio-cultural beliefs and rites is given in Robert E. Hood: *Must God Remain Greek?* Minneapolis: Fortress, 1990, pp.43–76.

3   The prayer 'Gentle Jesus meek and mild…' was taught to me and my three siblings by my own mother, in much the same way it was taught to Maureen and a number of Black people with whom I have spoken in this particular phase of the research project. She in turn was taught by her own mother, my grandmother.

4   A phrase in Jamaican creole that is a variant on the word 'mummy' or 'mother'.

5   A grammatical term in Jamaican creole meaning 'you' in the plural sense.

5

The impact of the oral tradition
Conversations on Black children

In order to develop this model further, I chose to work with two other families. This was to prove very instructive. The discourse that emerged from these conversations accorded with the developing themes from previous intergenerational sessions. Prayer remained an important component of the intergenerational discourse of these families. In ways that were remarkably similar to the first family, younger family members were taught to pray by their older relatives. As in the previous session the traditional prayer of 'Gentle Jesus', seemed to represent some form of signifier in connoting aspects of a Black religio-cultural heritage.

Another important theme that emerged from these additional conversations was the issue of 'otherness'. The cultures that emanate from Africa and the Caribbean remain persuasive and potent contributors to the identity formation of Black children and young people in Britain. (See Reddie 2000, Chapter 1). The children in these familial settings expressed an acute sense of engagement with the Caribbean and Africa, and the cultures that have emerged from these particular contexts.

The Caribbean remains a symbolic, dare one say romantic, construct in the minds of these Black children born and nurtured within pluralistic, inner-city contexts in Britain. The connectedness of Black children to the

Caribbean region is illustrated in the following conversation.

I met with Jonie, a Black woman in her early sixties, in October 1998. Jonie was a junior church/Sunday school leader in a Methodist church situated in the north of the city. Alongside Jonie was her granddaughter, called Debbie, and two great-nieces named Shona and Bonnie respectively. Debbie was six years old. Her two cousins were eight and six years old at the time of these structured conversations.

I began by asking the three young children for their thoughts on Jamaica, the birthplace of their grandmother and great-aunt.

> *Anthony (A)* [*to the three young girls*] So tell me. Have you ever heard of Jamaica?
>
> *In unison* Yeah.
>
> A   You all have. So Debbie, what have you heard about Jamaica?
>
> D   That they talk a different, like, accent.
>
> A   Yeah.
>
> D   And they play loads of drums.
>
> A   Ah. They play drums! And what is the weather like?
>
> D   Hot.
>
> A   Hot? Have you ever been to Jamaica?
>
> D   No.
>
> A   Seen pictures?
>
> D   Yep.
>
> A   OK. Have you ever heard anyone speak with the accent?
>
> D   No. Sorry.

A   No, no, it's. OK. [*To Bonnie*] Bonnie, what have
        you heard?

B   I've heard that it's really hot and errm, errm, they
        grow lots of crops and they don't get that much
        rain. And they've got, errm, they live in hotels
        and they're really, really posh. And that errm, the
        schools are quite big. The end!

A   Shona!

S   When the crops grow they have carnivals and
        make costumes for a month. And when they've
        made it they go on the streets playing drums and
        they go [*begins to sing a well known Caribbean
        Calypso song*] 'Are you feeling hot, hot, hot'. [*The
        other two children begin to join in.*] 'Feeling hot, hot,
        hot.' [*Stops singing.*] And with the wavers they go.
        [*Begins to wave her arms in the air, and is followed by
        her sister and cousin.*] And at school we learnt about
        carnivals.

A   OK.

S   And the steel bands came.

A   And steel bands came as well? OK. This question
        is for anyone now. What do you think is the
        biggest difference between being in Jamaica and
        being here? Anyone?

B   I think the biggest difference is because you've
        got all kinds of religions in this country, but I
        think you've just got Black in Jamaica.

A   OK. Debbie?

D   I think it's not that hot, and they've got like
        different houses.

A   OK. That's a good answer. And you, Shona?

S   I think they've got big studios, like pictures and,
        and, those studios. In Jamaica. I've heard about. I

know that, in Jamaica they have these big studios
and you see lots of people in there.

What is fascinating about the young girls' perceptions of
Jamaica is how far myth, popular culture and somewhat
clichéd images from the media have shaped their consciousness. Television, with its propensity for representing the
Caribbean as a romantic idyll for affluent tourists, has propagated an image of this region in general and Jamaica in particular that is one-dimensional in the extreme.

The girls focused their thoughts particularly upon music,
identifying drums and singing as being integral aspects of
Caribbean life. Incidentally, it should be noted that the
image of people making costumes in celebration of the crops
being harvested is more properly a socio-cultural phenomenon belonging to Trinidad and Tobago, and Barbados. The
song sung by Shona with the accompaniment of her sister
and cousin is by a well-known calypso/Soca singer called
'The Mighty Sparrow'. The song is part of the staple diet of
most Black parties, dances or celebrations. Calypso/Soca
music is not usually seen as part of the landscape of mainstream popular music in Britain. Its exposure on mainstream
commercial radio stations remains somewhat limited.

That these girls are familiar with this song is indicative of
their exposure to and link with African and Caribbean
cultural practices. Their familiarity with this music
emphasises the ability of young children to perceive and
construct notions of 'other' and 'difference'. Bonnie's perceptions of the differences between Jamaica and Britain were
an interesting conflation of religion and 'race'. She felt that
there were more religions in Britain (meaning a greater
pluralism), but there was only Black in Jamaica. Whilst one
might perceive Bonnie's comment as being a product of her
limited cognitive skills, I wonder how many adults in Britain
indulge in a similar kind of analysis? The conflation of 'race,'

ethnicity and religion appears to be a commonplace occurrence, and has been the subject of a great deal of study, particularly by the Warwick Religious and Educational Research Unit, University of Warwick (see Jackson and Nesbitt 1991; Nesbitt 1990; Jackson 1989, 1995).

We should not be surprised that Bonnie has conflated 'race' with religion, given the ways in which the Christian faith has been so closely aligned with European cultures and White power for several centuries (Reddie 1998b, pp.5–6). Bonnie recognises the difference between a country that is populated predominantly with Black people of African descent, and a more pluralistic country such as Britain. Intriguingly, Bonnie did not perceive Britain as a country of one religion, but of many. This, I believe is a positive development in the identification and recognition skills of this young child. Could this be the result of a more pluralistic, world religions approach to religious education?

These British-born Black children were aware of the Caribbean region. This awareness oscillated between seeing this region as a socio-cultural and historical reality and, conversely, as a romanticised, mythical 'other'. The two extremes of this continuum are influenced, if only marginally, by the opportunities afforded some of these children to visit this region for themselves. In the following discourse, the twin themes of socio-cultural and historical reality and romanticised myth are displayed in equal measure.

The following conversation involved Charlene and Terry and their respective older relatives. Charlene, who was fifteen when this structured intergenerational conversation took place, was a member of a Methodist church situated towards the western border of Birmingham. Terry, aged seven when this conversation took place, was also a member of this church. My conversation with Charlene and Terry was undertaken in November 1998. Alongside Charlene was her mother, Diane, plus Mel (a junior church/Sunday school leader along with Diane) and her husband Mick. Terry was the only son of Mel and Mick.

I began by asking the three adults for their memories of being nurtured in the Caribbean. Having heard the accounts of Diane, Mel and Mick, I attempted to ascertain from Charlene and Terry their thoughts and experiences of the Caribbean. The comments of the younger family members were supplemented by the older individuals. These comments were often made in very humorous terms, recounting embarrassing episodes from the recent past. I was struck by the sense of shared experiences between successive generations of Black people living in Britain.

> *Anthony (A)* So Charlene, you were born in Birmingham? [*She responds by nodding her head.*] Have you ever been to Jamaica?
>
> *Charlene (Ch)* Yeah.
>
> *A*   What did you think was the biggest difference between Jamaica and here?
>
> *Diane (Di)* Shall I tell you what she said?
>
> *Mel (M)* Apart from the weather!
>
> *Di*   When she got over the initial shock. 'Mum they're Black'! [*There is much laughter at this point.*] How old was she then?
>
> *M*   This was the first trip then?
>
> *Di*   First trip? Nine? Was it ninety? She was about six. And the first reaction? [*Pause.*] I think it's because she's used to seeing a lot of white people. And then you go, and everywhere you go, are Black people.
>
> *M*   [*interrupting*] Especially living in Rowley Regis innit, where we are? Because not a lot of Black people 'round here. I think in the whole of

Rowley there must be about, at a push, probably twenty families innit? At a push.

Di   Her first reaction was, I think, apart from as I said the heat, was the colour of the people. Not that she wasn't used to seeing Blacks you know, but she wasn't used to seeing so many in one place. [*There is more laughter.*]

A   [*to Charlene*] When was the last time you went?

Ch   Hmmm. Two?

Ch & Di Two years ago.

A   What was the biggest difference then? Being a little bit older?

Ch   I don't know. All the insects and bugs and stuff.

A   [*not quite hearing first time*] All the …?

Ch   Bugs.

A   Oh yeah. Yeah.

Di   [*begins to mumble under her breath*] The nightmares with the insects.

Ch   I don't know.

M   What about the difference between you as a teenager and the teenagers there?

Di   There isn't that much difference really.

Ch   No.

Di   They're all sort of … [*interrupted by Charlene.*]

Ch   Kinda like American.

Di   Jamaica seems to be very American.

Mick Of course, it's just 'round the corner.

M   That difference isn't really there. But I think as they got older they adapt more to change. Got used to the dogs and cats [*laughter*] and the cows in the yard a bit more. [*More laughter.*]

A   [*to Charlene*] Did you enjoy yourself?

Ch   Yes.

A   What was the best thing about it? Being there? Alright, not the best thing. Anything. Tell me, anything? Anything that you liked?

Ch   The beaches. [*Lots of laughter. Being very ironic:*] It's a bit better than Blackpool. Only a bit better.

M   What you mean a bit better?

Ch   A tiny bit better than Blackpool.

M   Get away. [*More laughter.*]

A   So Terry, have you ever been to Jamaica?

Terry (T) Yeah.

A   Did you like it?

T   Yeah.

A   What did you like?

T   Going on the motorbike.

A   [*in astonishment*] Motorbike? Oh gosh. What was the weather like?

T   Hot.

A   Hot. Hotter than over here?

T   No, Yes.

Ch   I don't remember it being hotter over there. Oh, I get what you said now. It is hot.

Di   'Gimme my sun glasses Mum' as soon as we got off the plane. 'Where's my sunglasses, where's my sunglasses?' [*More laughter.*] Blinded by the sun. 'I can't see, I can't take it.'

M   That's true. When we went two years ago innit?
         Hmm, I spent quite a lot of time with my eyes
         squinched up. And even with sunglasses on. I
         think next time I go I shall have to invest in a
         decent pair of sunglasses. Yes, it's a bit hard on
         the eyes when you're not accustomed to it. [*More
         laughter.*]

In a later part of the conversation I was struck by Charlene's
knowledge of her mother's formative years in rural Jamaica.
Charlene accepted that her mother's upbringing might have
been more tranquil and less complicated than her own
childhood. Nevertheless, she recognised that her own
formative experiences in Britain lacked the acute poverty of
her mother's early years. The shared experience of which I
spoke earlier has allowed Charlene and to a lesser extent
Terry to possess the Caribbean as a symbolic and signified
resource for their individual quest for a positive self-identity.

I believe that African-centred curricula and any related
discourse can assist Black children to gain a sense of their
otherness (see forthcoming Reddie 2001/2). These overt,
self-conscious attempts to assist Black children to access
their socio cultural and religious heritage are hugely important. Black elders, the greater majority of whom had their
formative experiences in this setting, are a crucial resource in
assisting Black children to gain a sense of the historical
dimension of their identity.

These transatlantic journeys were concretised within their
emotional and psychological frameworks through exposure
to these forms of familial remembrances. The importance of
Black cultural components and expression can be seen in the
connectedness between these forms and traits, and Black ex-
istential experience. Within the oral discourse of Black
people, notions of identity and selfhood are played out

against an ongoing repertoire of cultural frameworks whose antecedents are found in the continent of Africa.

Through the structure of intergenerational discourse it was my hope that the cultural expressions and experiences of Black people would be affirmed. Perhaps the resulting experiences and expressions of faith might enable children and young people from these backgrounds to gain a clearer sense of their own heritage. It is vital that succeeding generations of children gain a greater sense of engagement with the familial and corporate narratives of Black experience. Opportunities for these kinds of exposure and growth may provide beneficial outcomes in the emotional development and the maturing of faith within these children.

The importance of sharing African-centred stories of faith and experience is immense in overcoming the historic evils of miseducation and negativity that have been unleashed upon Black people over the past five centuries. These intergenerational conversations offer an additional, non-text-based approach to educating Black children into the cultures and heritage that have shaped their forebears.

I would argue that unless faith communities, social agencies, policy makers and educators begin to appreciate and affirm the wisdom and experience of Black elders, we will have failed to build upon the pioneering work of such luminaries as Carter G. Woodson, to whose pioneering work the historical development of a Black, African-centred perspective on the educational needs of Black people owes much. Woodson has been identified by many as the father of 'Black history'. His work has had an immense influence upon succeeding generations of Black scholars in the United States of America. His two seminal works (Woodson 1919/1990a and Woodson 1933/1990b) have provided the platform for more recent developments in African-centred approaches to the education of Black people.

Woodson outlines the historical developments in the education of Black people in the United States. Slave owners initiated these educational efforts in the first instance. Later efforts were led by abolitionists and philanthropists until the emergence of educational initiatives established by Black people themselves. The latter developments provided the antecedents for the growth and influence of the Black majority educational sector in the United States of America. This sector is manifested in schools such as Moorehouse and Spelman,[1] as well as in colleges and universities. (Woodson 1919/1990a).

Woodson asserted that the post-reconstruction education of Black people was characterised by a systematic and concerted effort to miseducate people of African descent. This period witnessed a cynical and manipulative attempt to permit the advancement of a relatively small number of Black people in the professional and commercial classes. These individuals were used, subsequently, to legitimate a discriminatory system that suppressed and exploited the overwhelming majority of Black people (Woodson 1933/ 1990b). He maintained that most Black people were educated by the State to believe that they were inferior, and were duly socialised into accepting an accompanying status. By controlling the thinking of the individual, the state was well positioned to control the mass of Black people in the country (*ibid.*).

The influence of Carter G. Woodson has been keenly felt in the educational discourse surrounding Black people in the United States of America for the greater part of the last century. Diana Slaughter contends that Black people have been miseducated within the various branches of the education system in the United States of America. She argues that Black children and young people have been perceived historically as a problem and have been educated with these racist, ideological pathologies constantly to the fore (Slaughter 1975, pp.10–19).

Slaughter's polemic calls for an educational process that juxtaposes the Black Christian experience within the black church in a progressive visualisation of the teaching and learning process. In short, Slaughter is arguing for a process of Christian learning which operates within a Black, African-centred framework that normalises and affirms Black experience and existence. This educational process contains an ideological strategy for the teaching and learning enterprise. By using the term 'ideological', I am asserting that such an approach to education adopts a partic-ular world-view in which one's commitment to the world and the belief structures held by the individual is consistent with their perspective on how the world should be ordered. This ideological stance is juxtaposed with a dialogical teaching strategy that engages Black youth with the histori-cal developments in their cultural identity. This latter point is fundamental to the education of Black youth in that it promotes an ongoing dialogue of mutual respect between those who are notionally being educated (children and young people) and those who teach them, namely adults (Slaughter 1975, pp.12–16).

Slaughter's work finds echoes in the progressive develop-ments advocated by Faustine Jones-Wilson. Jones-Wilson provides a concise analysis of historical developments in African American State education in America since the Second World War. She argues that African Americans must be well informed on educational issues in their country. Edu-cationalists, parents and members of the different Black communities in the United States of America must be aware of the ever-changing discussion that surrounds this often-times contentious area of public debate (Jones-Wilson 1990, pp.31–49). This debate has been sharpened, of late, by the continuing discussion surrounding the tax-dollars of 'hard-working' Americans, with particular reference to the appropriate levels of spending in urban deprived areas most frequently populated by minority ethnic people.

A previous generation of writers has argued that Black children require specialised programmes of education to assist them in their development. Donald Henderson and Alonzo Washington, for example, maintain that the unique nature of Black culture in the United States has resulted in Black children being nurtured into highly different behavioural and cultural norms that are not synonymous with white, Anglo-Saxon middle-America. As a direct consequence of these crucial differences, the authors argue that such factors as Black culture and history should form the basis for alternative curricula for Black children (Henderson and Washington 1975, pp.353–60).

Around the same time that Henderson and Washington were developing their approaches to the education of Black children, Ivory Toldson and Alfred Pasteur were creating a six-stage process of self-discovery for Black people. The work of these two educators was an attempt to counter the notion of Black self-negation. Arising from the ongoing negative representation and demonisation of Blackness by White authority, many Black people have developed a survival mechanism that is based upon a sub-conscious denial of the apparent source of their troubles, namely their very Blackness. The six-stage programme advocated by Toldson and Pasteur moves from the initial separation of the Black individual from nature and self, through to a positive affirmation of the individual's emotional and psychological appreciation of their Blackness. In colloquial terms, this sixth stage is indicative of the ability to state, unequivocally, that if I were to be created all over again from scratch I would still want to be Black, for to be Black is to be beautiful and precious. The authors advocate an educative process that incorporates the use of Black cultural and aesthetic art forms as a means of promoting this developmental process (Toldson and Pasteur 1975, pp.130–8).

The work of the aforementioned educators needs to be supplemented by the formational influence of Black elders. Faith communities, in particular, need to develop inter-generational strategies for education and nurture, that utilise the experiences of older people in a positive fashion.

The notion of an all-encompassing, intergenerational process for nurture and socialisation has been promoted by Jane Hilyard. She asserts that a corporate, intergenerational programme should include the specific intention of enabling children and young people to appropriate the family narrative, and consequently gain a positive affirmation of self (Hilyard 1979, p.106). Hilyard proceeds to outline a systematic process of Christian education rooted within the faith community that attempts to work on a number of levels – from the position of the individual within a family towards an intra-family model, and then onto an inter-family perspective. The teaching and learning process is intentional and informal (*ibid.* pp.108–15).

This approach to affirming and recognising the importance of the oral traditions of African elders represents a very real attempt to stimulate progressive developmental changes, in terms of psychological and emotional growth in Black children. The importance of these forms of proactive interventions for inner-city churches, collective Black communities in particular, and wider society in general should be self evident.

Outcomes and themes from
this section of the research

The oral tradition of Black elders can be a resource for the spiritual development, Christian education, nurture, and general emotional and psychological development of Black children. There are a number of caveats, however, of which we need to be conscious if we are to use this tool as a resource for Black children.

One of the major issues we need to address is the inherent tension between a critically reflective model of teaching that calls for an open, dialogical method between adult and child, where both are co-learners, and a more didactic, instructional process.

David Day's contention is that oral teaching sits uncomfortably with our more progressive notions of participatory, dialogical learning (Day 1992, p.167). Oral traditions tend not to reflect our seemingly enlightened notions of adults and children as co-learners in the teaching and learning process. Equally, oral traditions do not necessarily reflect the desirability for modernists of explicit reciprocity and the remaking of knowledge between co-learners acting in dialogue, as advocated by one such as Paulo Freire (Freire 1972, p.98).

It is interesting to note that the historical figure of Jesus is often perceived by many Christian educators and theologians as their model for an enlightened pedagogical process. Closer inspection, however, of the methods employed by Jesus would seem to reflect a more didactic, instructional model, where the recipients of his wisdom are more than likely to be passive observers, struggling to come to terms with his sometimes obscure use of allegory.

Moreover, Christian formation and general socialisation that emerges primarily from an oral tradition has tended to be most effective in situations that might be described as being homogeneous and compact (Mitchell 1986, p.100). Homogeneous and compact settings are contexts where there is a self-sameness and a shared experience among people of one dominant ethnic or racial group. In the United States, the Black church has most notably provided the basis for this communitarian ethic for people of African descent.

In Africa, evidence for these settings is even more plentiful (Soyinka 1990, pp.13–38). Similarly, within the Caribbean region, there are numerous examples of these socio-cultural settings (Erskine 1981 and Davis 1990). With suitable qualifications, one can make the case for the existence of these homogeneous and compact settings in Africa, the United States and the Caribbean (Asante 1990, pp.3–12).

Conversely, the diverse communities where Black people live in Britain could never be described as either homogeneous or compact. In pluralistic situations where a multiplicity of identities and experiences are in evidence, can one reasonably expect an oral tradition to be a realistic resource for the development of spirituality, Christian education and the general nurture of Black children? Can oral traditions cope in a realistic fashion with the disjunction and disparities in Black experience in millennial Britain?

The document I have created entails a dialogical method, whereby children and young people are encouraged to share their experiences with older members of the family. In order to explain the significance of this method, I will make recourse to a musical metaphor that might assist us in our understanding. This metaphor has proved useful on a number of occasions in helping me to conceptualise the nature of Black experience and the development of Black identities in twenty-first-century Britain (see forthcoming Reddie 2001/2).

The method inherent within the oral tradition parallels one where older members of a family or faith community seek to assist younger members to become acquainted with the musical culture of the people to whom they belong. Oral transmissions are concerned with replicating that tune or melody from one generation to the next.

Many of the adults with whom I worked would want younger family members to learn the melody in a very precise and deliberate fashion. There are a number of problems in attempting this course of action, as I will outline in a moment. Despite the dificulties in attempting to pass on the musical culture of the people, it remains imperative, however, that these younger individuals faithfully reproduce the integrity of the melody in a manner that both respects and reflects the historical deveolpment of the music.

In diverse, pluralistic settings in Britain, however, I am concerned that the musical culture of the people should be not replicated but improvised. Efforts at replication may prove impossible in contexts radically different from the settings in which the music first emerged. If replication is rejected, each new generation is encouraged, not so much to re-learn the melody in a static fashion, as to affirm its own contextual improvisations. The melody remains authentic to the experiences of Black people, but each generation plays the music in a fashion that reflects the reality of the contexts in which they live. This process of improvisation is assisted by Black people of different ages entering genuinely into intergenerational dialogue. This dialogical method aims to preserve the oral traditions of Black people, whilst giving real credence and space to the emergence of new experiences that are a part of the reality of being Black in Britain. It is my hope that the practical schema I have created will be a helpful tool for Black adults in their attempts to nurture a positive sense of self within their children and young people.

The importance of Black elders lies in their unique position as people who represent the pivotal link between a 'world that was' and the 'world as it is today'. These older Black people have lived in two remarkably different contexts. Their formative influences were shaped by the religio-cultural world of the Caribbean. This was a world of poverty and struggle, but equally (and perhaps more important), a world of belonging, affirmation and identity. If the metaphor of jazz music, where the improvisational qualities of young Black children are explored and enhanced, is to be valid, then we as a society must begin to affirm the status and value the wisdom and experiences of Black elders. It is their experience, memory and notions of lived faith which will provide the basis of the inherited melody, from which the improvisational process can emerge. In short, if Black elders are not encouraged to share their stories of faith and experience, there will be no melody from which their successors can learn. We need to encourage Black elders to tell their story to their grandchildren and great-grandchildren.

Strategies for undertaking intergenerational storytelling

These intergenerational conversations, I believe, are of potentially great significance in the identity and faith formation of Black children and young people. As we have seen from brief extracts, these sessions enable young Black children to become more conversant with their cultural heritage and history. The 'otherness' of their existence, or the plural nature of their identity, was restated. For children whose immediate or more distant parentage has emerged from varied locations in the world, gaining access to a range of stories and experiences that will influence their identity is of immense importance (see Cummins 1996).

One of the principle difficulties in enabling Black children and young people to gain access to their forebears' experiences and stories of faith is the disparate, fragmented nature of family life in Britain. The notion of the extended family, where several generations of one clan or familial grouping live in close proximity to one another, is largely a feature of the past.

One of the important arenas that provides opportunities for Black people of different generations to meet is, undoubtedly, the church. The following figures relate to the early statistical breakdown of the 'population' that constituted the research on which this book is based. As you will deduce from the research, inner-city churches and the Black people who attend them do represent a significant arena in which intergenerational discourse and interaction takes place in Britain.

Early statistical breakdown based upon the 26 churches in the study

Methodist 14

Anglican 6

URC 3

Bapist 2

Independent Pentecostal 1

The children

- 80.73% of children attending these inner-city churches were of African descent (18% are white European, 1.27% 'other'[2]).
- Of the junior churches/Sunday Schools at the above churches, 35% are comprised entirely of Black children.
- In 95% of the churches in the study at least 65% of children attending their junior church/Sunday School are Black.
- Children rarely attend junior church/Sunday School after the age of 14.
- The male to female ratio was 51.5% female to 48.5% male.

- The males are less likely to be members of junior churches/Sunday Schools after the age of 12.
- 80% of children have been baptised.
- 69% of the children attend with a grandparent (most usually a grandmother).
- 36% of the children attend with a parent.
- 55% of the children live within a three-mile radius of the church they attend on a Sunday

The first few bullet points are particularly instructive, as they show conclusively the numerical ascendancy of Black children in inner-city churches in Birmingham. The figures confirm the general socio-economic and demographic trends that have evolved in inner-city areas over the past twenty-five years.

In a significant number of churches (35%) there are in existence junior churches/Sundays schools that are comprised entirely of Black children. In the vast majority of these churches (95%) there was a minimum of 65 per cent of Black children attending junior churches/Sunday schools. A general maxim has been expressed on a number of occasions by ministers and lay leaders of the various churches in the Birmingham area, namely, that without the presence of Black people in these inner-city churches, many of these faith communities might not exist.

In the context of this book, great importance should be placed upon the figure indicating the high percentage of Black children brought to church by a grandparent. The apparent meeting point between older and younger members of most Black communities in inner-city churches in Birmingham (which is usually replicated across the major metropolitan conurbations of Britain) provides invaluable opportunities for Black children and young to learn from their forebears. Churches need to make and create greater opportunities for children to gain access to the stories of faith and experience of their elders. This can be undertaken within specific settings where children's learning takes place, or within the wider context of the whole church in which people of all ages are participating in corporate worship.

Alternatively, within more secular settings, various statutory and voluntary agencies can, perhaps, establish relationships with local churches. Might there be opportunities for children and young people to visit residential and nursing homes or sheltered housing provision, using the methodology I have developed in order that intergenerational conversations might take place? This suggestion, as I know from personal experience, is neither a new or a particularly startling proposal. As a university student many years ago I was part of a group of Methodist students (members of the Methodist Society, or Meth. Soc.) that travelled regularly to a Methodist Homes for the Aged establishment, to share in conversation with older members of the community. Those occasions were invaluable learning opportunities for all the students. I hope that our visits were ones that brought a sense of dignity and self-worth to these individuals and were not seen as a charitable exercise on our part. I am sure that we gained more from these interactions than our older counterparts.

Relationships between schools, churches, statutory and voluntary agencies need to be strengthened. We need to find ways in which the elders of our community and their younger counterparts can have greater contact and exposure to one another. Within the context of this work the storytelling festival highlighted in the following chapter was an important intergenerational context that brought people of all ages together. It is incumbent on all agencies and bodies to find ways of bringing people of different ages together.

Romney Moseley argues for a process of nurture that is not only intergenerational, but is also intercultural. Commencing from an African-centred perspective, Moseley argues for a process that enables Black youth to make connections between themselves and people of other cultures and situations who are struggling with oppressive structures not dissimilar to their own (Moseley 1989, pp.95–6). Within the context of intergenerational work I would argue that there is much merit in bringing not only people of different generations together, but also undertaking that task from an intercultural perspective. Such a process, argues Moseley, has the potential to create important links between disparate groups of people who may perhaps find that they have more in common than they formerly believed to be the case.

My final point in this chapter is somewhat fanciful, but the human spirit is infinitely impoverished if we cannot dream or indulge in flights of fancy. 'bell hooks' (this is the author's preferred presentation of her name), in citing Martin Luther King's notions of a 'Beloved Community', speaks of a place where all people are affirmed. This community is one where racism, sexism, classism and ageism are absent, and all people are afforded the dignity they deserve as individuals created in the image of God, irrespective of race or creed (hooks 1996, pp.10–11). This dream may yet find fruition, assisted by the structure of intergenerational conversation outlined in this work! In theological terms, this dream is the practical commitment to realising the Kingdom of God.

Notes

1   Moorehouse and Spelman are male and female single-educational schools located in Atlanta, Georgia. They are widely regarded as being amongst the best Black majority educational institutions in the United States of America. Their alumni include many of the great African American personalities and

achievers. Moorehouse's greatest alumnus is arguably the Revd. Dr. Martin Luther King, Jnr.

2   This figure includes children of South Asian descent (Hindus and Sikhs originating from India), African descent (Ghana and Nigeria) and Chinese descent (China and Hong Kong).

6

Implications for the work with elders in Britain

Working with Black elders

A number of years ago, prior to my involvement with the Birmingham Initiative, I worked for short time within a social services community care team for the elderly. As a social work assistant I visited a number of elders in their homes and in social-services-run residential homes. Given the catchment area covered by this team, I came into contact with a number of Black elders, the majority of whom had travelled from the Caribbean to Britain in the 1950s and 1960s. Whilst a number of the individuals I met seemed relatively contented with the situation and circumstances in which they found themselves, a larger proportion were somewhat dissatisfied and disaffected.

The latter were troubled at the sense of isolation and marginalisation they were experiencing at this late stage of their life. Many of them had not come to Britain in order to grow old, or to die. A number of these individuals harboured intense hopes of returning to their homeland to spend their remaining years in the sunshine idyll of their youth. Given that many had come from relatively small rural communities in the Caribbean, the shock (for some) and disappointment of feeling isolated in their own home or in a residential home was a heavy psychological burden to bear. Even after all these years, I remember still the words of one elderly woman in her late seventies, living in a residential home, stating that,

> Young man, back home, we wouldn't even treat a mangy dog the way they treat old people over here. Dese dey [these] people, dem not even like dem own, what sey ol' coloured [the term 'Black' is the more accepted word in common usage now] people like we? Laard, 'elp coloured people who find demselves in dis dey cold place.

Reflecting upon these comments I am at pains to stress that they in no way represent an indictment of the workings of the social services department in this large metropolitan council. The comments of this woman, I believe, represent a more generic perception of Britain as a country that does not value its older members. We give the impression that economic function and utilitarianism are the main criteria for the value and the importance we confer upon particular individuals and certain groups of people. Those who are able to make a significant, financial contribution to the nation are lauded and applauded. Conversely, those unable to make such a tangible contribution are deemed to be inferior, perhaps second-class, even surplus to requirements. One only has to reflect upon the language that is invoked when we talk about people who are unemployed. These individuals are often perceived as 'lazy scroungers', 'dossers' and 'freeloaders'. Governments, of whatever persuasion, know that they can appeal to the small-minded, utilitarian, 'they should pay their way' mentality of the electorate by appearing to 'get tough' with those who are without work. If your worth within society is judged on the economic contribution you make, is it any wonder, then, that those without work will be pilloried and disparaged?

The fact that elders have already made their economic contribution does not shield them from the harsh assessment that, at this precise moment in time, they are an economic burden. They are no longer making that necessary, called for, contribution. Hence, we disparage them, albeit in benign and emollient tones, but disparage nonetheless.

The importance of this work, for the country as a whole, but particularly, for those agencies charged with working alongside Black elders, is the necessity of taking seriously the wisdom and experience of these individuals. Whilst I was engaged in this work I was reminded constantly of the poignant words of that older woman in the residential home. If Britain pays scant regard to older white people, what, then, will be the fate of the increasing number of Black elders? They belong to the *Windrush* generation that has grown old in this country, and for an increasing number the completion of their life will be in this country also. What of them? How can British society as a whole, including the church and her many partner agencies, meet the challenge of working creatively with Black elders? This research work has highlighted a number of important themes.

First was the importance of enabling Black people to tell their story. These are stories of faith and experience that have given meaning to, and defined the existence of many Black elders. They are the stories of struggle. The stories of determination and overcoming. Stories that have shaped the Black post-Second World War experience in Britain. Stories that have enabled me to be here today undertaking this work. How can we affirm these stories, and what will be the effect of our doing so? I will deal with the second question first.

Affirming the stories and experiences of Black elders

It is a general truth that self-esteem rises if you perceive yourself as a person of worth. If your very presence and what you say matters to others, then undoubtedly you feel affirmed and have a greater belief in your own worth. The converse, of course, is also very true.

One of the worst indictments I can level at this country has been our seemingly casual disregard of the experiences, stories and contributions of Black people in this country. It would be both churlish and remiss of me not to acknowledge the important, dare I say, prophetic work undertaken by the Methodist Church in this area. Publications like *News from Notting Hill* (Mason, Ainger and Denny 1967), *People,. Churches and Multi-Racial Projects* (Holden 1985) *A Tree God Planted* (Walton 1985), *Faithful and Equal* (the Methodist Church 1985) and (with a certain air of modesty) my own work in *Growing into Hope*, and the invaluable work of the Methodist and Ecumenical Leadership in Racism Awareness Workshops (known as Melraw) and the Racial Justice Office of the Methodist Church, have all contributed to raising the profile of Black people in Britain.

I would not want to give the erroneous impression that the Methodist Church was alone in offering a prophetic voice in this area. One needs to consider the important work of the Church of England and a number of her landmark documents, of which *Seeds of Hope* (Church House 1991) and *A Passing Winter* (Church House 1996) are among the most notable.

In the wider society there have been publications, documentaries, dramas and exhibitions that have documented aspects of the Black experience in Britain, but these have been fleeting and transitory. On the whole, Black people in Britain have been largely invisible, save for the rhetoric and vituperation surrounding minority ethnic people with reference to matters of immigration and asylum seeking.

One of the most striking things to emerge from this section of my research was the sense of affirmation and confidence many of these individuals gained simply from the fact that an 'official' person wanted to converse with them about their experiences. I remember one woman saying, 'Why do you want to talk to me? Me is not anyone special.' I countered, 'You are special, because your story is special. You're special to God, so it is an honour for me to speak with you.'

The challenge for all agencies working alongside and with Black elders is to find ways in which they can encourage these individuals to share their stories of faith and experience. The oral traditions of people of African descent have their origins in Africa. Many of the traditions and the cultures that have shaped their lives are thousands of years old. Yet because of the effects of racism and marginalisation the manifestations of these oral traditions, contained in the form of stories of faith and experience, have rarely been given an opportunity to be expressed and affirmed in a public setting. Often the liturgies and theological reflections that are reflective of the mission and the ministry of the church are so grounded within a Eurocentric framework that they exclude the experiences and cultures of Black people.

In order to connect emotionally, spiritually and psychologically with Black people, it is essential to understand the world-view that influences and, in part, defines people of African descent. From my interaction with these elders I have seen that they are profoundly religious people. The blandishments of secularism and humanism have not penetrated their existence. The world of the spirit and the evidence of their spirituality and Christian convictions are very publicly on display.

If you reread the earlier chapters you will gain a clear sense of the spirituality and Christian world-view of African people in general and Black elders in particular. Theology occupies a prominent place within the philosophy of Black elders. Peter Paris has commented on the theological expressions of African people, which permeate every aspect of their life (Paris 1995, pp.27–49). To understand, and then work

effectively with Black elders, one has to realise the importance of, and become conversant with, the Christian
religious discourse that flows through their lives. God is
both immanent and transcendent. In effect, God is close at
hand, assisting believers in their daily struggles. Yet that
same God is far away, beyond the immediate struggles of the
world, overseeing the whole created order, beyond all space
and time. For Black elders, the secular and the religious
co-exist in the one time and space. The 'here and now' and
the 'hereafter' exist in the one continuum. The spirit world
and the material world meet (Paris 1995, pp.51–8; Hood
1990, pp.183–244). These Black elders possess the facility
to hold in tension the seemingly compartmentalised and the
apparently contradictory. Theirs is a world of miracles and
the ordinary – often, miracles within the ordinary, a world of
the spirit and the flesh. It gives eschatological hope for the
future, a belief in the final and complete fulfilment of God's
reign in the world to come. Yet, conversely, this firm convic-
tion sits alongside a strong belief that justice and righteous-
ness should be fought for in the harsh concrete realities of
this world.

A criticism that can be levelled at a number of organisations and agencies in their attempts to work with Black
elders is that their practice rests upon social scientific
theories and models which are secular in character. Whilst
there are many merits to this approach, its very perspective
and the assumptions that follow from it are often at variance
with the experiences and spirituality of the very people they
are attempting to serve. One cannot work effectively with
Black elders unless there is an appreciation of the theistic
grounding of their existence. To put it bluntly, you cannot
divorce Black people from God.

For those agencies that do acknowledge the theistic
element, it is not sufficient to develop liturgies and theological reflection which assume that White European perspec-

tives are the norm. Whilst these Eurocentric notions of God and the accompanying expression of the Christian faith and spirituality are more in keeping with African concepts of existence than, seemingly, social scientific secularism, they nonetheless still fail to engage meaningfully with Black experience. Agencies such as the Church and her many sister organisations need to become conversant with the lived experience and the folk theologies of people of African descent. (See Mitchell 1975.) To understand Black elders, one needs to understand the world from which they have emerged and the stories of faith and experience that have shaped them. By acknowledging oral traditions that have given rise to these stories, and the historical sources and experiences from which they have emerged, agencies will become more effective in their work. Of equal importance will be the affirmation and self-esteem Black elders will derive from having an opportunity to share their stories of faith and experience.

How to facilitate the stories and experiences of Black elders?

I do not want to give the impression that I possess a number of guaranteed strategies for facilitating the stories and experiences of Black elders. What I can offer are examples and suggestions.

Undoubtedly the most important way in which individuals, agencies and organisations can encourage and gain access to these stories and experiences is through the medium of pastoral care. There are a number of publications that can assist practitioners in gaining a greater understanding of the emotional, spiritual and psychological needs of Black people (see Wimberly, E.P. 1979, 1991, 1999; Lartey 1997).

Without wishing to lose ourselves in great detail, for this is a somewhat complicated matter, practitioners and policy makers need to be aware of a crucial caveat when dealing with this issue. (See my forthcoming publication *Nobodies to Somebodies*, Reddie 2001/2.) Due to the effects of racialised oppression and marginalisation, many Black people may well be suspicious or even reluctant to talk in depth about personal stories or experiences. This reluctance will be exacerbated if the person seeking to initiate or facilitate the conversation is a White European. The sense of alienation and disaffection felt by Black people over the past five hundred years (from our forced removal and captivity in slavery, through to the period of British/European colonialism and imperialism of the more recent past) has manifested itself in a number ways. One particular manifestation has been the tendency of Black people to submerge or disguise aspects of their existence and experience from the wider world which, often dominated by White people and their concerns, was viewed with suspicion (see Reddie 1998b, pp.7–9 and 1998c, pp.8–10). In order to gain access to those experiences and stories, one will need to exercise a great deal of patience. It may take some time for Black elders to become familiar with the notion of sharing their stories. Many of them may not have had a previous opportunity to share their experiences with people outside of their immediate circle.

Practitioners will need to display humility and exude a sense of genuineness and integrity when engaging with Black elders. In time, however, when a rapport has been established, individuals who once might have been quite diffident may become sufficiently confident to share their stories of faith and experience.

See Appendix for a training exercise I have used with ministers and lay people offering pastoral care to Black elders, and also with many health care professionals in the secular voluntary and statutory sectors.

In addition to patience, one will need to develop the skill of persistence. It may well be the case that people who have been overlooked and marginalised for some length of time will view attempts to get them to share aspects of their lives with some suspicion. Some may hold the view that, 'By their fruits you shall know them' – if this person really wants to hear my story, then they will ask again. Black people are more than familiar with the tokenistic, cursory appeal to our better natures, which is underpinned by nothing more than paternalistic good intentions and a placating of one's conscience. Too many times I have heard the rather pathetic excuse, 'Well, I asked him or her.' Yes, you did. But if that person has been made to feel invisible and worthless for countless numbers of years, why should they suddenly wish to speak with you? Are they to be grateful? Are you really that important? The need for persistence can be irritating and time-consuming, but nevertheless, it is the only approach that will attest to one's genuineness and integrity.

In attempting to encourage Black elders to share aspects of their experiences, perhaps the most significant event in the course of my research within the Birmingham Initiative was the 'Storytelling Festival'. This event was held at my home church, Moseley Road Methodist Church in Birmingham, to mark the end of my work with the project. The stories from the many participants who took part in this final stage were acknowledged and affirmed in a more public setting, within a storytelling festival. The festival was organised by me and the many people who had played an active part in the research. The churches associated with the project were invited to this community evening. Many of the participants who had made a significant contribution to the research were present and shared a number of short extracts from the intergenerational conversations they had undertaken with me. The event was not dissimilar to a corresponding community event in the previous year at which *Growing into Hope* had been launched.

The storytelling festival was a significant event in that it represented an important occasion when the often privatised experiences of Black people were presented in a public arena. These stories of struggle, oppression and liberation took centre-stage and were duly affirmed. A number of the stories shared on that evening reminded me of the story I had written in a previous publication, using the experiences of an older African Caribbean women as a paradigm (Reddie 1998c, pp.28–31). In this story, entitles 'This Is Her Life', I invented an archetypal Caribbean woman in her early seventies, called Raphelita. Having constructed the narrative of her life, I divided the story into 16 parts. Adult leaders

---

The Birmingham Initiative
Storytelling Festival
19 June 1999

(1) Anthony Reddie to introduce. What the evening is all about!

(2) Anthony Reddie: a short monologue about growing up in Bradford.

(3) MRM Soul and Spirit (Moseley Road Methodist Church singing group): one song.

(4) Who is the oldest person you remember in your family? What were they like? Can you think of one story or incident you have heard about them?

(4a) Group participation. Turn to your neighbour and tell them who is the oldest person you remember in your family.

(5) The young people from Lozells Methodist Church perform 'All change' from *Growing into Hope*.

(6)   Bonnie sharing her knowledge of all the books of the Bible – taught to her by her grandmother.

(6a) Jonie (Bonnie's grandmother) telling us about coming to England.

(7)   Mel: Growing up in Ja. And then coming to England.

(8)   Jillian Brown: Personal reflections and poetry*

(9)   MRM Soul and Spirit: two songs

BREAK FOR FOOD. IN ORDER NOT TO FINISH LATE, IF YOU COULD EAT AND RETURN IN 30 MINS. SIT IN YOUR GROUPS AND TELL EACH OTHER ABOUT YOUR EARLIEST MEMORIES OF GROWING UP. WHAT DID YOU ENJOY AND WHAT DID YOU NOT ENJOY?

(10) MRM Soul and Spirit: another song to kick us off.

(11) Bee and her family: earliest memories, important people, trying to support one another.

(12) Youth Group from Lozells Methodist Church performing 'Freedom' from *Growing into Hope*.

(13) Lyn talking about the differences between her mother, herself and Lasharna. (Do this as part talk, part interview.)

(14) Group participation: turn to your neighbour. One of your happiest moments.

(15) Beverley Greaves: her experiences.

(16) MRM Soul and Spirit leading the finale. Repeating songs if necessary.

* Jillian Brown died on 7 October 1999. The piece she read at this event is published in *Legacy: Anthology in Memory of Jillian Brown*, ed. Anthony G. Reddie. Peterborough: Methodist Publishing House, 2000. pp. 58–62.

working with Black children and young people were invited to mix up the 16 sections and to ask their young learners to re-assemble the story into it's correct order. The story of Raphelita's life surved as a paradigm for Black struggle and emancipation.

I feel that events like a storytelling festival (an outline of which appears above) can assist churches and other agencies in enabling Black elders to share their stories, in order that their life experiences can be validated and affirmed.

A framework for generic work with elders

This research with Black elders has a wider generic application beyond the initial group with whom the work was first conducted. I believe that my investigation into the oral traditions of Black elders has resonance and applicability for those working with and supporting elders from a variety of ethnic backgrounds and cultures.

What are the implications of this work for those working with elders in Britain? The answer to this question, I believe, lies in the framework I have developed in the course of this research. If you cast your mind back to Chapter 3 and the development of the document 'Sharing stories between people of different generations,' you may recall the process that gave rise to this piece of work. My concern to devise a mechanism that would allow Black people of different generations to engage in familial conversation led me to develop this document. Examples of its use were given in Chapter 4.

While the preceding research and subsequent framework of 'Sharing stories between people of different generations' were devised specifically to initiate and support inter-generational storytelling, the utility of this method can be applied to dedicated work with elders per se. I believe that the initial research and reflections which led to the document lend themselves to generic work with elders in a number of varying contexts.

It is very important, in developing this form of work with elders, to understand the cultures and the contexts in which the people with whom you are working have been socialised and nurtured. Undertaking this process of research and reflection is vital, if you hope to create both a structure and an ensuing content that will resonate with the experiences and narratives of your client group. Charles Foster, a renowned theologian and Christian educator, has emphasised continually the importance of pastors and leaders of faith communities being able to 'read' the narratives of faith that connote meaning amongst any corporate group of individuals (see Foster 1982, 1987, 1994).

In the context of this work I undertook a great deal of theological reflection and research into the relationship between experience, faith and narrative with reference to Black people. In the course of this investigation I was able to develop the different sections and themes contained in 'Sharing stories between people of different generations'. It may be that these sections and themes are generic ones, appropriate for work with elders in different contexts and backgrounds from those in which I worked when conducting this research. This, however, may not be the case, and so it is important for practitioners wishing to use the model I have developed to adapt and amend it for the individual contexts in which they work.

This model for initiating conversation may enable elders to reconnect with their past and with one another. The past decade or so has seen a renewed interest in reminiscence work, in addition to the use of professional storytellers and oral history projects, all aimed at stimulating and affirming elders in this country. Reconnecting people with their past and affirming the significant moments in their life are hugely important tasks for all persons and agencies charged with caring for and supporting elders.

This document has been developed to help elders of their respective communities to reflect upon and retell the important incidents and pivotal moments in their lives. Its structure is intended to provide opportunities for elders to share their stories of faith and experience in order to gain some measure of self-esteem and connectedness with others. In addition to enhancing self-esteem and mutuality with peers (and the younger generation), this method accords with the central tenets of faith development theory, particularly the work of James Fowler *et al.* (See Fowler 1981, Fowler *et al.* 1980, and Fowler *et al.* 1991.) Developmental psychologists and practical and applied theologians assert that faith develops and mutates in response to ultimate questions of existence and meaning over the course of an individual's life.

I believe that this particular method of initiating discussion with elders from a variety of backgrounds and cultures, and the content generated by this approach, may enable ministers, pastoral visitors and health care professionals to gain insights into the substantive issues of faith for elders.

Given the isolation that is a common experience for many elders, I believe that the framework of this approach to oral traditions may provide an important mechanism for dispelling depression and despair. From my own work with Black elders, I have been amazed at the resilience and fortitude of so many of our older citizens.

Prior to creating this method of initiating structured conversations, my fascination with the anecdotal qualities of personal storytelling and their effect on me led to the creation of 'This is her life', an exercise in the 'Mothering Sunday' section in *Growing into Hope* (Reddie 1998c, pp.29–31). The exercise was written for older children and those in their young teens. It consists of a printed sheet on which is a series of rectangular boxes. Inside each box are brief details recounting the life experience of an older Black woman. The facilitators/leaders working with the children make photocopies of the page, cut out the boxes, shuffle them, and then place them in a pile. The children are asked to reassemble the boxes in the correct chronological order, thus putting the woman's life back together. In addition to the obvious challenge of reconstructing a linear narrative that represents this woman's life, the children are asked to reflect upon its content. What has the woman learnt over the course of her life?

This activity and other exercises and stories in that section of *Growing into Hope* (*ibid.* pp. 14–38) were inspired by the stories of the many elders I had met during the course of my research prior to the oral tradition work. While my studies at the time were concerned with the impact this form of traditional wisdom and biographical narrative exerted upon Black children, I witnessed also the effect of this work on the elders themselves. A number of the Black elders rejoiced at the opportunity to share aspects of their story with others. The sense of mutuality and connectedness to one's past, and to the peers with whom the past is shared, became powerful factors in the collective learning experience that resulted from many of these sessions.

A number of the Black elders with whom I worked remarked that they felt an increased sense of value and worth through having the opportunity to share their stories of faith and experience with others who 'knew what it was like'. I am reminded of the thoughts of Norman Jones, an African Caribbean man in his late fifties. Norman had hoped to share his story at the storytelling festival in June 1999, but other concerns prevented him from attending this event. Norman wrote the following words and sent them to me prior to the storytelling festival. He was reflecting upon his own story, which he had shared as a member of the fellowship group at a Methodist church in the northwest of the city. (I refer to this group in the section entitled 'Speaking with Black

Elders: An early attempt' at the beginning of Chapter 2.)
Norman said:

> Telling my story to the others reminded me that one of the
> most important aspects of my faith is that of my
> background and culture. I am a Black person and a Black
> person who originally came from the Caribbean. I am
> aware of my background and the history of my people, who
> came from the Caribbean. We are all descendants of slaves.
> For myself and for all Black people, whether we come from
> Caribbean or African backgrounds, or have family in the
> Caribbean and Africa, we need to remember that we have
> been given the gift to be ourselves. We are children of God.

I am convinced that the insights derived from this section of
the research are equally applicable to the many diverse communities and peoples that constitute this nation. If Norman
and his peers felt affirmed and energised through sharing
their stories in a supporting and affirming setting, I have
reason to believe that others, in whatever context they find
themselves, might benefit from this type of initiative.

Using the experience of Black elders as a resource for the Christian education and spiritual development of the younger generation: the value of intergenerational storytelling

The educational possibilities of this area of work lie in the
potentialities they provide for the emotional development of
Black children. Michael Clarke states that one of the primary
difficulties facing young Black people in their development
is the discontinuity that exists between them and their past.
He writes

> I have noted that in our developing technological society
> there has been a significant shift from the past, especially in

the transmission of faith. No longer are the elderly the transmitters of stories; in fact there is little dialogue between the youth and the aged. (Clarke 1995, p.4)

Clarke asserts that the fragmentary nature of contemporary urban life has led to an all too apparent divergence in diasporan Black life. This is manifested in the discontinuity between African peoples of differing generations. Clarke continues: 'We must discover ways to pass on our stories, stories that tell us who we are, stories that will help individuals to continually discover God's presence in their lives' (*ibid.* p.4). Through exposure to the narratives and expressions of faith of their forebears, black children gain access to survival strategies and aphoristic wisdom that might assist them in their individual struggles. The impact of this form of intergenerational oral tradition work upon Black children and young people is demonstrated in the discussion with the family in Chapter Four. The latter part of that discussion provided opportunities for family members to indicate briefly their sense of hope for the future. (See also the final section of the document 'Sharing experiences between people of different generations' in Chapter Three.) In this portion of the discussion it became clear that Lesley's own hopes for the future were buoyed by the very real support and affirmation she had gained, and continued to receive, from older members of her family.

The conversations in this intergenerational session gave me an opportunity to gain a sense of the educational opportunities that might accrue from this non-text-based approach to Christian education. It is instructive to note that when I asked Maureen for comparisons between her own faith and that of her mother, she felt it was difficult to arrive at accurate conclusions. Aside from the qualitative judgements called for in such comparative analysis, Maureen said, 'We haven't really sat down and discussed our faith as such … I don't know. We haven't discussed it.'

The lack of formal discussion about matters of faith and personal narratives should not surprise us. The differentiated nature of modern life and the fragmented, even isolated experience of family that affects many individuals have led to myriad patterns of familial existence (E. P. Wimberly 1999, p. 17). Even a family as close as this one meets in its entirety only once a week on a Sunday. There are many families for whom even this limited opportunity for a corporate sense of oneness is not possible.

Within many Black families in Britain there are many issues related to the ongoing struggles for familial cohesion and a sense of corporate identity. We should not forget some of the current realities at play in present-day Britain. This is a context where lives are governed by the all-pervasive influence of postmodernism. The old assumptions surrounding family life are fast disappearing. In this particular era the realities of social and geographical mobility are constantly challenging the traditional notions of family cohesion. In light of the aforementioned factors, the opportunities afforded this family through the structured oral tradition schema were of great importance.

The oral tradition document was developed as a practical and theoretical piece of work, building upon the literature and the previous developments in *Growing into Hope*. This schema enabled this family to engage in a focused type of conversation, which might not have taken place were it not for the intervention of the research project. It is my belief that these forms of intergenerational conversation, although there may be an element of contrivance in their application, nevertheless perform an important function. This form of structured discourse facilitates the preservation of familial narratives and historical and socio-cultural experiences. Fred

Lofton amplifies the importance of retaining the collective and corporate experiences of African people when he writes:

> Each family must pass on to the next generation the family tree, the heritage, the traditions, and the causes for celebration. The Black family has a special mandate to do so because of past injustices and the failure to preserve much of our group culture. (Lofton 1991, p.129)

The wisdom and experience of Black elders, I believe, provide a hugely important resource for the spiritual development and general nurturing of faith amongst a younger generation of potential believers. While written text in the form of Christian education programmes of learning and worship will always remain important models of teaching, the wisdom and experience of the *Windrush* generation is a diminishing resource. I believe it is vitally important that we find ways of affirming and utilising the skills, experiences and knowledge of this generation of people. The transatlantic migratory travels of the *Windrush* generation were a vast sea of Black humanity on the move, fuelled by specific economic, sociological and historical forces. It was a specific moment in time, the like of which will not occur again in that particular form. We need, therefore, to treasure these people – for the struggles they have been through, for their fortitude and graciousness in the face of seemingly insuperable odds. Their role and function in Britain has been to act as a reminder to a racist country that the Christian faith is larger than the mean, myopic spirit of racism and White supremacy that greeted many of them upon their arrival here in the 1950s and 1960s (Reddie 1997).

Indeed, I am of the opinion that the presence of a largely God-fearing community in Britain at that time reminded a so-called Christian country that we are called to love God with all that we possess and to love our neighbour as ourselves. Despite innumerable provocation and trials, Black elders have stood the test of time. Many of the churches that once offered welcomes imbued with suspicion and hostility are now communities of faith that would no longer exist were it not for that self-same, once disparaged and demonised group of people.

I believe that Black children and young people, in fact the whole country, should be rightly proud of the achievements of these people. Their stories of faith and experience need to be told, and the various branches of the church in Britain, and the many other agencies that offer support and care to Black elders, need to listen and learn. We will all be the better for having had access to the remarkable legacy of faith of African peoples, which are contained within the oral traditions dating back to the earliest moments in human history. The stories of faith and experience of Black elders in Britain are the latest chapters to be added to an ongoing story that is as old as time itself.

I hope that this book is a useful addition to our collective knowledge and appreciation of those who paved the way in order that I and others like me might be here. To these people, especially my parents, I owe so much that the debt will never be paid. My mission is to educate those who will nurture the young, in order that they can retell this story to the generation that will follow them, so as to ensure that it is never forgotten. This book is for my ancestors and my decendants!

Appendix

'How do I feel?' A training exercise

The following exercise was created in order to illustrate the means by which Black elders have been disempowered and silenced in a process that has seen older African and Caribbean people rendered speechless and seemingly inarticulate, lacking an authentic voice. This process has been manifested in implicit and explicit forms. 'How do I feel?' is an experiential attempt to enable pastoral carers, health and social care professionals and policy makers to 'climb into the skin' of Black elders in order to gain a brief sense of how and why this denial of a voice takes place. Ways of overcoming this ongoing struggle of Black elders for visibility and affirmation are offered in the section entitled 'How to facilitate the stories and experiences of black elders?' in Chapter Six.

The exercise

Give each person a piece of paper on which is written one of the two following statements.

> - You are stupid, backward and useless. Everything you do, or think, is inferior and without merit. You feel embarrassed about anything you do, and cannot bear doing anything in public in front of other people. You must not reveal this fact to anyone else.
> - You are a natural born leader. Everything you do is correct. You have supreme confidence in who you are. Everyone agrees with you and supports your way of doing things. There is nothing you cannot do. You must not reveal this fact to anyone else.

1. Leaders should shuffle the slips of paper thoroughly before handing them out. Hand out both statements at random. (It is important that the group receives equal numbers of both slips.)

2. Having handed out the slips, ask the group to sit in a circle. You then pretend to have a Bible study. You can choose any passage you wish. My suggestion is **Luke 5: 1–11, Jesus calls the first disciples**. For more secular settings, any text with which the participants are reasonably familiar, and from which a number of questions can be asked, is applicable for this exercise. Ask questions related to the passage. The questions should be in two broad categories. Vary the questions between the first and second types.

    • Questions directed at the whole group. You ask a general question, and wait for volunteers to give any possible responses. You encourage anyone to respond, but only those who are described in Statement Two should answer. If someone described in Statement One answers, find a very obvious way of discrediting the answer or point that they have made.

    • Questions delivered to individuals. Choose individuals at random, and ask them very basic questions on the passage. Some will answer readily, others will be more reticent.

3. After ten minutes or so ask the group what they have noticed. Who spoke and who did not? Why did some people speak, and why did others not feel able to speak? Groups can now reveal the true

reasons for their behaviour. Those who were without confidence and self-esteem – how did they feel? Was it frustrating? Dispiriting? What about those who were allowed to be confident? How did they feel?

Reflections on the exercise

This exercise is intended to show how particular roles and labels, when imposed upon certain people, deny them the opportunity to express themselves and reveal their authentic selves. This has been the continued legacy of four hundred years of slavery and colonialism. Black people have been told repeatedly that they were inferior, without value, importance or worth.

This indoctrination has seen millions of Black people internalise their sense of inferiority to the point where many of them reject or submerge aspects of their real selves and identity (in terms of culture, attributes and spirituality) in favour of what they see as superior European norms and values. We need to be aware of this if we are to meet the needs of Black elders and younger Black people. In attempting to empower and inspire them with the confidence to see themselves in positive terms (proud of their culture, history and heritage), it is imperative that various agencies charged with working alongside Black elders see spirituality and the Christian faith as important factors in their work. If such agencies and individuals relegate this facet of their work to the periphery, then Black elders will never feel like 'whole' people. It is unlikely that they will feel comfortable and at ease with their identities in the context of institutional or more informal caregiving situations. In theological terms Black elders (like all humankind) have been created in the likeness of God. As such they remain as vital a part of God's creation as every other human being on earth.

While the exercise and following reflections have, like the majority of this book, taken as their focus Black elders' experiences and stories of faith, the generic applicability of this exercise should not be lost. While I would argue that a sense of marginalisation and displacement is particularly acute for black elders and has deep echoes and resonance with colonial history, it accords to some degree with the experience of all elders.

As I have highlighted in this final section of the book, societies that are predicated on notions of utility and economic function are not usually ones in which the voice of the powerless or the marginalised are heard. In more prosaic terms, if you are perceived as having no valid, productive, economic contribution to make to the wider society, then why should your voice be heard?

It is interesting to note that since the advent of 'grey power' or the 'grey vote' in many western societies, the respect accorded to older citizens has grown exponentially. While there is much at which we can rejoice, in relation to the increased respect accorded to older citizens, and the increased time that politicians are affording them, this burgeoning importance does not disprove the basic thesis of my argument. British society cannot yet claim to extend an 'elder-friendly' ethos in terms of its treatment of and attitude towards elders, Black or otherwise.

The advent of 'grey power' testifies to the mobilisation of elders as an electoral force in British democracy. If they had not mobilised their efforts, I suspect that the Chancellor of the Exchequer would still believe that pension increases amounting to less than one pound per annum are acceptable.

On occasions when the exercise described above has been used in training and awareness-raising sessions, I have found that the irritation of those who receive the first statement quickly turns to agitation and even downright anger. This agitation and anger becomes all the more pronounced if they are professional, articulate, White, middle-class individuals. Social workers and ordained clergy are very bad performers in this exercise, particularly if they are exposed to the first statement. Are there any reasons for this state of affairs? Can we deduce from such observational analysis an inherent psychological flaw in the people who make up the social work profession and the ranks of the ordained clergy?

In fairness to these two groups of professionals I would assert that failure to engage in a playful way with the contrived dynamics of this exercise, does not reflect any innate failings on the part of social workers or ordained clergy per se. Rather, it offers us a reminder of, and perhaps an insight into, the institutional power and influence such groups exert upon others. This exercise, and the reactions of various people to it, addresses the sense of control and 'having one's voice heard' that exists within each discipline. Social workers or ordained clergy, each in their own particular field, exert enormous amounts of influence and even power. Such individuals would not be human if, in the course of their work, they did not develop an acute sense of 'being able to ensure that your voice is heard'. Whether through case conferences or sermons, they are offered ample opportunity to be heard, and for their opinion to be accepted as valid.

Given such conditions and circumstances in one's work, imagine the shock at suddenly being rendered mute! The freedom to articulate or vocalise one's emotions, views, beliefs or preferences is suddenly denied. The effect, even within an exercise that is 'make-believe', can be dramatic. In this exercise the disparity between the White, middle-class and professional and the Black, elderly, and marginalised is starkly represented. Those who represent the former need to respect, affirm and identify appropriate ways in which to empower the latter. I believe that this book has described a methodology and resulting schema ('Sharing experiences between people of different generations') that offer an important tool for enabling practitioners and policy makers to do just that.

References

Allen, W. R. (1982) 'The search for applicable theories of black family life'. *Journal of Marriage and the Family 40*, 117–30.

Asante, Molefi Kete and Asante, Kariamu Welsh (eds.) (1990) *African Culture: The Rhythms of Unity*. Trenton, NJ: Africa World Press.

Aschenbrenner, J. (1978) 'Continuities and variations in black family structure'. In Shimkin, D. Shimkin, E. and Frate, D. (eds.) *The Extended Family in Black Societies*. Chicago, IL: Aldine.

Aschenbrenner, J. (1980) 'Extended families among black Americans'. *Journal of Comparative Family Studies 4*, 257–68.

Bailey, Randall C. (1991) 'Beyond identification: the use of Africans in Old Testament poetry and narratives'. In Felder, Cain Hope (ed.) *Stony the Road We Trod: African American Biblical Interpretation*. Minneapolis: Fortress Press.

Beckford, Robert (1998) *Jesus is Dread: Black Theology and Black Culture in Britain*. London: Darton, Longman and Todd.

Berryman, Jerome (1991) *Godly Play*. San Francisco, CA: Harper San Francisco.

Birchett, Colleen (1989) 'A history of religious education in the black church'. In Rogers, Donald B. (ed.) *Urban Church Education*. Birmingham, AL: Religious Education Press

Bruce, Calvin E. (1976) 'Black spirituality, language and faith'. *Religious Education 72*, 4.

Carter, Harold A. (1984) *The Prayer Tradition of Black People*. Baltimore, MA: Gateway Press.

Clarke, David (1995) *Reclaiming the Black Experience in the Anglican Church of Barbados: A Study Among a Group of Young Anglicans*. Unpublished D. Min. thesis. Trinity College, Ontario, Canada.

Cone, James (1975) *God of the Oppressed*. San Francisco: Harper San Francisco, CA: Harper Collins.

Connerton, Paul (1989) *How Societies Remember*. Cambridge: Cambridge University Press.

Crockett, Joseph V. (1991) *Teaching Scripture from an African-American Perspective*. Nashville, TN: Discipleship Resources.

Cummins, Jim (1996) *Negotiating Identities: Education for Empowerment in a Diverse Society*. Ontario, Canada: California Association for Bilingual Education.

Curry, Bonita Pope (1991) 'The role of the black church in the educational development of black children'. In June, Lee N. (ed.) *The Black Family: Past, Present and Future*. Grand Rapids, MI: Zondervan Publishing.

Daniel, Jack and Smitherman-Donaldson, Geneva (1976) 'How I got over: communication dynamics in the black community.' *Quarterly Journal of Speech 62*, February.

Davis, Kortright (1990) *Emancipation Still Comin'*. New York, NY: Orbis Books.

Day, David (1992) 'Apples of gold: the role of proverbial wisdom in Christian education'. Astley, Jeff and Day, David (eds.) *The Contours of Christian Education*. Great Wakering, Essex: McCrimmons.

Denis, Phillippe (1995) 'The use of oral sources in African church history'. *Bulletin of Contextual Theology 2*, 1. Cape Town, South Africa.

Diop, Cheikh Anta (1974) *The African Origins of Civilization*. Chicago, IL: Lawrence Hill Books.

Du Bois, W. E. B. (1965) *The World and Africa*. New York, NY: International Publishers.

Erskine, Noel (1981) *Decolonising Theology*. New York, NY: Orbis Books.

Foster, Charles R. (1982) *Teaching in the Community of Faith*. Nashville, TN: Abingdon Press.

Foster, Charles R. (1987) 'The pastor: agent of vision in the education of a community of faith'. In Browning, Robert L. (ed.) *The Pastor as Religious Educator*. Birmingham, AL: Religious Education Press.

Foster, Charles R. (1994) *Educating Congregations*. Nashville, TN: Abingdon Press.

Fowler, James W. (1981) *Stages of Faith.* San Francisco, CA: HarperCollins.

Fowler, James W., Schweitzer, Friedrich and Nipkow, Karl Ernst (eds.) (1991) *Stages of Faith and Religious Judgement.* Birmingham, AL: Religious Education Press.

Fowler, James W., Berryman, Jerome and Keen, Sam (1980) *Trajectories of Faith: Five Life Stories.* Nashville, TN: Abingdon Press.

Frazier, E. Franklin (1964) *The Negro Church in America.* New York, NY: Schocken Books.

Freire, Paulo (1972) *Pedagogy of the Oppressed.* New York, NY: Herder and Herder.

Freyer, Peter (1984) *Staying Power: The History of Black People in Britain.* London: Pluto Press.

Goldberg, Michael (1982) *Theology and Narrative: A Critical Introduction.* Nashville, TN: Abingdon Press.

Hale, Janice (1994) *Unbank the Fire.* Baltimore, MD: The Johns Hopkins Press.

Hale, Janice (1995) 'The transmission of faith to young African American children'. In Bailey, Randall C. and Grant, Jacquelyn (eds.) *The Recovery of Black Presence.* Nashville, TN: Abingdon Press.

Hale-Benson, Janice (1986) *Black Children: Their Roots, Culture and Learning Styles.* Baltimore, MD: The Johns Hopkins Press.

Hall, Douglas (1981) *Free Jamaica: 1838–1865: An Economic History.* Aylesbury: Ginn.

Hannah, D. (1991) 'The black extended family: an appraisal of its past, present and future statuses'. In June, L. N. *The Black Family: Past, Present and Future.* Grand Rapids, MI: Zondervan.

Hazareesingh, Sandip (1994) 'Remembering the past: personal memories and family narratives'. In Hazareesingh, Sandip, Kenway, Penny and Simms, Kelvin (eds.) *Speaking About the Past.* Stoke-on-Trent: Trentham Books.

Henderson, Donald H. and Washington, Alfonzo G. (1975) 'Cultural differences and the education of black children: an alternative model for program development'. *Journal of Negro Education 44*, 353–360.

Hill, R. and Shackelford, L. (1986) 'The black extended family revisited'. In Staples, R. (ed.) *The Black Family: Essays and Studies.* Belmont, CA: Wadsworth.

Hilyard, Jane (1979) 'Family and intergenerational education'. In Perry, David W. (ed.) *Homegrown Christian Education.* New York, NY: Seabury Press.

Hood, Robert E. (1990) *Must God Remain Greek? – Afro Cultures and God-Talk.* Minneapolis, MN: Augsburg Fortress Press.

hooks, bell (1996) *Killing Rage: Ending Racism.* London: Penguin Books.

Jackson, R. (1989) *Religion Through Festival: Hinduism.* London: Longmans.

Jackson, R.(1995) 'Religious education's representation of "Religions" and "Cultures"'. *British Journal of Educational Studies 43,* 3, September, 272–89.

Jackson, R. and Nesbitt, E. (1991) *Hindu Children in Britain.* Stoke-on-Trent: Trentham Books.

John, Gus (1976) *The New Black Presence.* London: British Council of Churches.

Jones-Wilson, Faustine C. (1990) 'The state of African-American education'. In Lomotey, Kofi (ed.) *Going to School: The African-American Experience.* New York, NY: State University of New York Press.

Josselson, Ruthellen and Lieblich, Amia (eds.) (1993) *The Narrative Study of Lives, Vol. 1.* California: Sage Publications.

Lartey, Emmanuel Y. (1997) *In Living Colour.* London: Cassell.

Lofton, Fred (1991) 'Teaching Christian values within the family.' In June, Lee N. (ed.) *The Black Family: Past Present and Future.* Grand Rapids, MI: Zondervan Publishing.

Mbiti, John S. (1970) *African Religions and Philosophy.* New York, NY: Doubleday.

Mbiti, John S. (1975) *Introduction to African Religion.* London: Heinemann.

Melchert, Charles F. (1998) *Wise Teaching: Biblical Wisdom and Educational Ministry*. Harrisburg, PA: Trinity Press International.

Mitchell, Ella P. (1986) 'Oral tradition: legacy of faith for the black church'. *Religious Education 81*, 1, Winter.

Mitchell, Henry (1975) *Black Belief*. New York, NY: Harper and Row.

Moseley, Romney M. (1989) 'Retrieving intergenerational and intercultural faith'. In Foster, Charles R. and Shockley, Grant. S (eds.) *Working with Black Youth*. Nashville, TN: Abingdon Press.

Nesbitt, E. (1990) 'Religion and identity: the Valmiki Community in Coventry'. *New Community 16*, 2, 261–74.

Owusu, Kwesi (ed.) (2000) *Black British Culture and Society*. London: Routledge.

Paris, Peter J. (1995) *The Spirituality of African Peoples*. Minneapolis, MN: Fortress Press.

Prins, Gwynn (1991) 'Oral history'. In Burke, Peter (ed.) *New Perspectives on Historical Writing*. Cambridge: Polity Press.

Raboteau, Albert (1978) *Slave Religion*. Oxford: Oxford University Press.

Ramdin, Ron (1999) *Reimaging Britain*. London: Pluto Press.

Randle, Ian (1993) *Caribbean Freedom: Society and Economy from Emancipation to the Present*. London: James Currey.

Reddie, Anthony G. (1997) 'Exceptional prejudice?' (1997) In *The Risk Kit: God-centred, Challenging, Inspiring Practical Ways to Help the Renewal of Your Church*. Peterborough: Methodist Publishing House.

Reddie, Anthony G. (1998a) 'An unbroken thread of experience'. In King, Joan (ed.) *Family and All That Stuff*. Birmingham: National Christian Education Council.

Reddie, Anthony G. (1998b) *Growing into Hope I: Believing and Expecting*. Peterborough: Methodist Publishing House.

Reddie, Anthony G. (1998c) *Growing into Hope II: Liberation and Change*. Peterborough: Methodist Publishing House.

Reddie, Anthony G. (1999) 'The journey of a lifetime'. *Magnet 45*, Spring. London: Network.

Reddie, Anthony G. (2000) 'The christian education of Black children in Birmingham: Creating a new paradigm through developing better praxis.' Unpublished PhD thesis, School of Education, University of Birmingham.

Reddie, Anthony G. (forthcoming 2001) *Nobodies to Somebodies.*

Roberts, J.D. (1980) *Roots of a Black Future: Family and Church.* Philadelphia, PA: Westminster.

Shockley, Grant (1989) *'From emancipation to transformation to consummation: a black perspective'*. In Mayr, Marlene (ed.) *Does the Church Really Want RE?* Birmingham, AL: Religious Education Press.

Shorter, Aylward (1978) *African Christian Spirituality.* London: Geoffrey Chapman.

Slaughter, Diana T. (1975) 'The education of black youth as a cultural problem'. *Criterion 14*, Autumn, 10–19.

Soyinka, Wole (1990) 'The African world and the ethnocultural debate'. In Asante, Molefi Kete and Asante, Kariamu Welsh (eds.) *African Culture: The Rhythms of Unity.* Trenton, NJ: Africa World Press.

Stokes, Olivia P. (1974) 'Education in the black church: design for change'. *Religious Education 69,* 4.

Sudarkasa, N. (1981) 'Interpreting the African heritage in Afro-American family organization'. In McAdoo, H. (ed.) *Black Families.* London: Sage.

Thompson, Paul (1988) *The Voice of the Past: Oral History.* Oxford: Oxford University Press.

Toldson, Ivory L. and Pasteur, Alfred B. (1975) 'Developmental stages of black self-discovery: implications for using black art forms in group interaction'. *Journal of Negro Education 44,* 130–8.

Tonkin, Elizabeth (1992) *Narrating Our Past: The Social Construction of Oral History.* Cambridge: Cambridge University Press.

Vansina, Jan (1985) *Oral Tradition as History.* London: James Currey.

Walker, Robin and Biye, Kike O. (eds.) (1997) *1996 Black Community Report Vol. 2: 1997 Black Child Report.* London: Amenta Marketing Ltd.

Walton, Heather (1985) *A Tree God Planted: Black People in British Methodism.* London: Ethnic Minorities in Methodism Working Group, Division of Social Responsibility.

Werbner, Richard (1998) *Memory and the Postcolony: African Anthropology and the Critique of Power.* London: Zed Books.

Wilkinson, John, Evans Jnr., James H. and Wilkinson, Renate (1985) *Inheritors Together: Black People in the Church of England.* London: The Race, Pluralism and Community Group of the Board for Social Responsibility of the Church of England.

Williams, Eric. (1970) *From Columbus to Castro: The History of the Caribbean 1492–1969.* London: André Deutsch.

Wimberly, Anne S. (1994) *Soul Stories: African American Christian Education.* Nashville, TN: Abingdon Press.

Wimberly, Edward P. (1979) *Pastoral Care in the Black Church.* Nashville, TN: Abingdon.

Wimberly, Edward P. (1991) *African American Pastoral Care.* Nashville, TN: Abingdon.

Wimberly, Edward P. (1999) *Moving from Shame to Self-Worth.* Nashville, TN: Abingdon.

Woodson, Carter G. (1919, 1990a) *The Education of the Negro Prior to 1861.* Republished: Brooklyn, New York, NY: A & B Book Publishers.

Woodson, Carter G. (1933, 1990b) *The Miseducation of the Negro.* Republished: Trenton, NJ: Africa World Press.

Subject Index

Author Index